Sweeter Than Honey

A taste of the New Testament through 700 Questions and Answers.

Teryila Solomon Addi

SWEETER THAN HONEY - A TASTE OF THE NEW TESTAMENT THROUGH 700 QUESTIONS AND ANSWERS

First edition. May 23, 2019.

Written by Teryila Solomon Addi.

About the Author

Teryila Solomon Addi was born to the family of late Mr. Simeon Elias Ortyom and Mrs. Magdalene Hadiza Addi who have all received the supreme call to be with the Lord. He is the first of eight siblings and is in his late fifties. He was born in Kaduna, started primary school in Kano, completed in Jos and attended the prestigious N.K.S.T. Secondary School Adikpo. He worked with the Benue State Ministry of Agriculture but didn't reach the government required retirement age before leaving the service due to the Divine call into Missions. Since then, he has served in both the Para Church and Church organizations in different capacities. He holds PGDs in Animal Production, Educational Technology, Theology and a Master of Arts in Theology and Development Studies besides other short term courses and certificates. His marriage to Mrs. Shipinen Beatrice of about three decades is blessed with five children. He is currently pasturing with the Church of Christ In Nations (COCIN) and resides in Jos Plateau State.

Literature (PVT) Limited, Katunayake, 1992).

Acknowledgement

Immense thanks and praise to my Lord and Savior Jesus Christ who salvaged me from perishing, drew me to Himself and has made me share in His treasure and tribulation.

I am delighted to mention Reverends DaudaMaigari, Monday Zock, David Laje, Iwuji and Venerable HabilaArdzard who were my Pastors at various times and afforded me the opportunity to serve during their tenures in various capacities through which I got exposed and equipped for the ministry I have today.

Thanks to Reverend Matthew and Mrs. Rhoda Barde, Mr. and Mrs. Eli Gana, Mr. and Mrs. Daniel Shashere, Mr. and Mrs. Haruna Alkali who encouraged me in various ways during the compilation of this book.

Special thanks to God for my late siblings who prayed, helped and encouraged me during the compilation. To you Sister Nguzungwen Mercy, brothers Tarvenda Moses and Terungwa Abraham (Angel Addi) – you did not live long to see the production as it took time to come to fruition.

I specially thank God for my second half Evangelist Mrs. Shipinen Beatrice, our children Jennifer, Irene, Gift, Matthan, Micheal, Worthy and Joseph for perseverance during the period of putting this work together. I also appreciate my surviving siblings, in-laws, friends, their families and members of the churches I worked in through the years. You are all special instruments used by the Lord in shaping me. May he reward you abundantly.

Preface

Sweeter than Honey is written to enable the reader get deep into the New Testament of the Holy Bible.

It is aimed at taking the reader through the New Testament in various ways as evidenced in the nine chapters. The reader is expected to attempt supplying the answer(s) before looking them up in the answer section. It is recommended for Bible students of all levels, the young, the old, generally Christians and non-Christians alike who wish to taste the honey- like nature of the Word.

In my ministerial work in the Para church, the church and with students of secondary and tertiary institutions in West Africa, I observed a peripheral knowledge of the Word. In contrast, my interaction with people of other faiths revealed that they handle their scriptures with more seriousness and zeal in order to transmit same to subsequent generations. This became a burden to me and has led to the compilation of this book. I believe this book will not only be handy, easy to understand but also attractive and bring the reader into God's very presence and grace through its realities.

The Fill in the Gap section is meant to provide ready answers to some rhetoric questions often asked by some preachers. The True or False section and the Direct Questions are prepared to stimulate the reader into deeper meditation with an intention to analyzing and synthesizing the concerned scripture. Characteristics of people and places are meant to supply the reader with first hand tips about the character or place concerned. This can be a useful tool for both personal and group devotions. The importance of reciting scripture needs no over emphasis. Jesus defeated Satan through the Word (Luke 4:3-12). This section is meant for equipping the reader especially in our generation when scripture reading and recitation is waning in popularity among believers. Location and fulfillment of Messianic prophecies as found in the New Testament is also included just as the parables of Jesus Christ and their locations are here to equip the reader on the number and nature of Jesus' parables written in the New Testament.

I strongly uphold that the compilation and setting out of the elements of this book in such a simple manner which though not exhaustive but adequate, will draw many to Christ, have meaningful devotion and meditation as well as obtain skeletal information for sermon preparations and or general Bible Study from the New Testament.

Dedication

This book is dedicated to my daughters Jennifer, Irene and Gift Orty-omAddi. I pray they remain agents through which the world will have a taste of the Word.

Bibliography

SECTION ONE: QUESTIONS

This section contains questions asked in this Book, which are from Chapter one to Nine. The reader is expected to read each question carefully, think out the right answer before checking out the answer in section two.

Chapter ONE

FILL IN THE GAPS

This chapter has similarities with the chapter on recitation of content. Certain Bible statements are written and some part omitted in one or more gaps as provided in each question. It is expected that the reader will supply the missing parts as they appear in the Bible version used. It is intended to help the reader learn and know the scripture by heart in order to use it as a weapon in spiritual warfare just as Jesus Christ did in defeating Satan, as found in Matthew 4:1-11 and Luke 4: 3-12

It will help the reader know that sometimes, scripture is quoted by the enemy only to dribble one into falling. Knowledge of scripture will at such times help one counter such evil intent of the enemy as Jesus Christ did.

Please fill in the gap(s) with the appropriate answer (s).

1. .... is the recorder of the gospel of Matthew.
2. The sword of the Spirit in the book of Ephesians Chapter Six is the .... of God.
3. The location of Jesus' discussion with the Samaritan woman was ....
4. Before Stephen was stoned to death, the witnesses laid down their clothes at the feet of a young man called ....
5. Jesus Christ denounced the cities of ...., ... and ....where most of His miracles had been performed because they did not repent.
6. .... was chosen to replace Judas Iscariot.
7. .... rebuked Herod the Tetrarch because of Herodias,

his brother's wife.

8. Jesus Christ is the ...., ... and .... no one comes to the Father except through Him.

9. The Samaritan woman said "You are a Jew and I am a Samaritan woman. How can you ask me for ....

10. Besides Levi (Matthew), ...was also a tax collector whom Jesus Christ dined with.

11. .... men buried Stephen and mourned deeply for him.

12. Jesus Christ met and healed .... number of lepers as He travelled along the border between Samaria and Galilee.

13. Because there was plenty of water and many came to be baptized, John the Baptist baptized at ....

14. Demetrius was a silversmith who incited the people of .... to riot against evangelism.

15. .... and .... first discovered Jesus' empty tomb.

16. In order not to abandon one's faith, Peter in his Second Epistle said the believer has to ....

17. Apostle Paul says he is being poured out like .... and time has come for his ....

18. Sarah obeyed Abraham and called him ....

19. Marriage is to be honored by husbands and wives and the bed should be kept ....

20. As servants of Christ, we are entrusted with the ....

21. "And my God will .... according to His glorious riches in Christ Jesus".

22. Christ told his hearers that Moses allowed the Israelites to divorce because of the ....of their ....

23. The temple in the New Testament will be .... and ....

24. Apostle Paul and his companions were proud of the Thessalonian church for the following reasons ...., ... and ....

25. Believers are warned not to be unequally yoked with ...., because righteousness does not have fellowship with ....and what communion has light with ....

26. In his instructions on worship and advice to women, Apostle Paul says the woman will be saved through childbearing if she continues in ...., ..., ... and ....

27. God has chosen only .... alone to save mankind.

28. Salvation is obtained by confessing Jesus as Lord and ....whom God raised Him from death.

29. We should stop judging one another. Instead we should ....

30. Foolish and stupid arguments produce ....

31. Whoever turns a sinner back from his/her wrong way will .... and ....

32. A married woman is bound by law to her husband as long as

....

33. The new city does not need the sun or moon to shine on it but .... will give it light and .... is its lamp.

34. Every believer is saved by .... through .... and not a result of our works but God's gift so no one can .... about it.

35. God can dwell in one's heart through ....

36. Since I have been crucified with Christ, I no longer live but .... My bodily life is lived by .... because He loved me and gave Himself for me.

37. New believers are taught to put off the old self which is ...., be made new in .... and put on ....

38. If anyone does not take care of his relatives especially members of his own family, he has .... and ....

39. Apostle Paul said he fought a .... fight and......................... his race.

40. Bethsaida is the home town of ...., ... and ...., Jesus' disciples.

41. Those who hear the word and believe have already passed from ....to ....

42. Even though Jesus Christ came to give us life abundantly, Satan's intention has still been to ...., ... and ....

43. ...., a .... came to Jesus Christ by night asking Him how to be born again.

44. Jesus Christ being the Bread of Life, those who come to Him will neither ...., nor will those who believe in Him go ....

45. For a believer to bear fruit, he has to
....

46. Believers are justified through
....therefore we have
.... with God through Jesus
Christ.

47. Believers are advised to stop thinking as children but be
infants in .... and adults in
....

48. Rather than take solid food, the young believer needs
....

49. For .... sake, believers are told to submit themselves to
their earthly authorities.

50. With respect to forgiveness, ... and .... can
hinder spiritual growth.

51. The greatest in the kingdom of heaven must be
.... and become
....

52. The Book of Philippians states.......................... as one hindrance
to spiritual growth.

53. Believers are enjoined not to think of themselves more highly
than they ought, but rather, with .... in accordance
with the measure of .... God has given us.

54. Our love should not only be in words but must show itself in
....

55. Believers are told not to conform to worldly standards but
they should be ....,..............then they will test and
approve ....

56. Whether you .... and .... or .... you do,
do it all for the glory of God

57. Be ...., ..., be men of courage, be ...., do
everything in love.

58. As chosen people of God, believers must clothe themselves with ...., ..., ..., ...and ....

59. The Holy Bible encourages believers to work with their hands for reasons of .... and ....

60. A believer, having been enlightened, tested the heavenly gift, shared in the Holy Spirit and goodness of God who then backslides is .... and subjecting Him to public disgrace.

61. God resists the .... but gives grace to the ....

62. Unwholesome talk, immorality and love for riches all can hinder ....of a Christian.

63. Whosoever exalts himself shall be .... and he who .... himself shall be exalted.

64. The greatest among you should be like the .... and the one who rules, like the one who ....

65. Believers are urged to be humble in the sight of the Lord, and He shall ....

66. With respect to righteousness, ... can hinder one's spiritual growth.

67. Christ's humility is seen in His becoming man and being obedient unto ...., even death ....

68. Feet washing by Jesus Christ is one of His marks and teaching on ....

69. Elizabeth (mother of John the Baptist) wondered why she was so favored that .... should come to her.

70. The Samaritan woman was living with the .... husband when she met Jesus Christ.

71. John the Baptist was beheaded at the orders of ....

72. Believers are warned to ensure that no one misses the grace of God so that no .... root grows up to cause trouble and defile many.

73. The Holy city, the New Jerusalem will come out of heaven from God, prepared and ready like ....

74. The place / town where Jesus Christ healed Peter's mother in-law is ....

75. One of the two blind men healed by Jesus Christ is called ....

76. The demon-possessed man coming out from the tombs was healed by Jesus Christ at the region of ....

77. A man will leave his .... and .... and unite with his wife, and the two shall become one.

78. Jesus Christ asked His disciples whom people thought He is when they came to the region of ....

79. The man with dropsy was healed by Jesus Christ on .... day.

80. During the plan to kill Jesus Christ, before being anointed at Bethany, He along with His disciples withdrew and stayed in a village called ....

81. According to John's record, Jesus Christ escaped the grip of unbelieving Jews and went again ....

82. The crowd's first response after Peter's address on the day of Pentecost as recorded in the Book of Acts of the apostles was ....

83. Jude records that in the last times, there will be scoffers who will follow ....

84. Jesus Christ healed a man invalid for .... years in

Jerusalem at the pool near the................. gate.

85. Faith comes from .... and hearing the ....

86. Together with some of the elders, Ananias the high priest and ....a lawyer brought charges against Apostle Paul before Governor Felix.

87. The spiritual man makes .... about all things, but is not subject to man's ....

88. Man is not justified by observing the law but by ....

89. .... was the beggar who stayed at the gate of the rich man dressed in purple, fine linen and lived luxuriantly

90. When He ascended on high, he led .... in his train and gave .... to men.

91. Believers are to endure hardship as .... since God treats them as ....

92. As Jesus Christ is the ...., anyone that comes to Him will never go ....

93. The day will not come until the .... occurs and the man of .... is revealed.

94. Since the end of all things is near, believers should be clear minded and .... so they can ....

95. At the Pharisee's supper, Jesus Christ taught invited guests to a wedding feast, not to on their own take ....

96. The dragon in Revelation Chapter Twelve, swept a third of the stars with its .... out of the .... to the ....

97. Jesus Christ healed the two blind and mute men due to their ....

98. As recorded by John, some Greeks came to see Jesus Christ so first .... told .... and they both went to tell Jesus Christ.

99. On the resurrection day, following a violent earthquake .... came down from heaven, went to the tomb,

....

100. The woman on the beast in Revelation had a title on her forehead thus "Mystery of .... the great, the mother of .... and of the abominations of the earth.

Chapter TWO TRUE OR FALSE

These are a set of questions rooted from the Holy Bible, whose aim is to enable the reader know and appreciate differences between closely related concepts therein. They are meant to make the reader think carefully and not rush in supplying the answers.

Check the correct answer – True or False.

S/No	Questions	True	False
1	Jesus Christ healed a woman who had been crippled for eighteen years, on a Sabbath		
2	Annas was High Priest when John the Baptist ministered		
3	Amos, (not the Prophet) was an ancestor of Jesus Christ		
4	Levi was a tax collector before becoming an apostle of Jesus Christ		
5	Jesus Christ talked with the Samaritan woman at Samson's well.		
6	A priest travelling to Jericho from Jerusalem saw the man beaten, robbed and half dead. He therefore came, took him, bandaged his wounds and kept him in care of an inn-keeper and paid for his care while away.		
7	Nicodemus was a Pharisee.		
8	All the lepers healed by Jesus Christ came back to praise God.		
9	At the wedding in Canaan, Jesus Christ performed His first miracle		
10	On resurrection, Jesus Christ appeared to the eleven disciples the following day.		
11	While at Bethsaida, Jesus Christ sent out the twelve disciples		
12	Jesus Christ also paid taxes even though a King and Messiah.		
13	Jesus Christ cursed the fig tree		
14	Jesus Christ never taught in the temple		
15	Besides the five thousand, Jesus Christ also fed four thousand people miraculously		

16 In one of Jesus' miracles, He raised Dorcas from death

1.

2. S/No   Question True False

3.

4.

5.

6. A priest travelling to Jericho from Jerusalem saw the man beaten, robbed and half dead. He therefore came, took him, bandaged his wounds and kept him in care of an inn-keeper and paid for his care while away.

7. Nicodemuswas a Pharisee.

8. All the lepers healed by Jesus Christ came back to praise God.

9. At the wedding in Canaan, Jesus Christ performed His first miracle

10. On resurrection, Jesus Christ appeared to the eleven disciples the following day.

11. While at Bethsaida, Jesus Christ sent out the twelve disciples

12. Jesus Christ also paid taxes even though a King and Messiah.

13. Jesus Christ cursed the fig tree

14. Jesus Christ never taught in the temple

15. Besides the five thousand, Jesus Christ also fed four thousand people miraculously

16. In one of Jesus' miracles, He raised Dorcas from death

17. The disciples brought back to life the widow's son at Nain

18. The fig tree is reported to have withered at

Jesus' order

19. The seed that fell on stony ground died later due to lack of roots

20. The sword of the spirit is also the Word of God

21. Jesus Christ even ate and drank with sinners and tax collectors, contrary to Jewish beliefs

22. On the expiration of one thousand years, Satan will be loosed out of his prison

23. Jesus Christ is the vine while Christians are the main stem

24. Jesus' yoke is easy and His burden is light

25. Anyone who lacks wisdom should ask from God, who gives generously without finding fault and it will be given him

26. The Holy Bible recommends faith even where there are no works

27. Even though the world is sinful, God still loves it

28. In Christ, there is no male or female

29. Although Apostle Paul was a Pharisee, he was also a Roman citizen

30. Saul's conversion took place near Jerusalem on his way to persecute the Christians there

31. On conversion, Apostle Paul ministered in Arabia before coming to Jerusalem

32. Apostle Paul while in Athens, was greatly distressed, seeing that the city was full of idols

33. Lydia was Apostle Paul's convert at Thyatira (Philippi)

34. Jason was arrested instead of Paul and Silas because he not only housed them but also failed to produce them for arrest on demand

35. Though Timothy's mother was a Jew, his father was Greek

36. Physical circumcision was needless since he believed, so Apostle Paul just took Timothy along for ministry even though a Greek

37. Apostle Paul had a sister whose son overhead a conspiracy against him (Paul) in Jerusalem

38. Apostle Paul was detained in the prison at Caesarea for two years by King Felix

39. When you are persecuted in a place, do not flee to another, remain there.

40. Jesus Christ poured some little calm water into the raging stormy sea to calm it before finally rebuking it.

41. The Holy Bible states that spirit-filled Christians can cleverly serve two masters.

42. Christians are encouraged to apply the law of 'eye for eye' and 'tooth for tooth' when pushed to the wall.

43. Jesus Christ quickly visited and rescued John the Baptist when He heard of the later's imprisonment.

44. The Magi reported to King Herod after discovering and worshipping the child – Jesus Christ.

45. "Are you the one who was to come or should we expect someone else". John the Baptist

asked this question when Jesus Christ visited him in prison.

46. All the cities in which Jesus Christ performed most of his miracles repented.

47. Jesus' brother, sister or mother is whoever does the will of his father in heaven.

48. The disciples were not afraid when they saw Jesus Christ walking on water.

49. Jesus Christ answered and healed the Canaanite woman's daughter instantly as she came.

50. Faith in God as little as the size of a mustard seed can move a mountain.

51. The Lord promises to be present where two or three come together in his name.

52. The gospel shall be preached in the whole world as a testimony to all tribes before the end will come.

53. Apostle Peter denied Jesus Christ only two times before the rooster crowed.

54. Pilate reluctantly handed Jesus Christ over to the Jews for crucifixion.

55. Levi's occupation before becoming a disciple of Jesus Christ was also fishing.

56. Jesus Christ went to the seaside and called his disciples.

57. John the Baptist was beheaded on Herod's birthday.

58. Out of fright, Peter requested for three shelters on the Mountain of Transfiguration.

59. Jesus Christ drove people out of the temple because they made it a den of robbers.

60. Couples will still to marry themselves at resurrection because what God has joined together, nothing shall separate.

61. Jesus Christ was anointed by a woman who came with an alabaster jar of very expensive perfume made of nard at Capernaum.

62. Jesus Christ promised going ahead of his disciples into Galilee after his resurrection.

63. Simon of Cyrene who was forced to carry Jesus' cross was also the father of Alexander and Rufus.

64. When Jesus Christ was nailed to the cross, there was extra ordinary brightness from the sun as from the sixth to ninth hour.

65. Joseph, husband of Mary, mother of Jesus was a descendant of David.

66. Zechariah and Elizabeth disagreed at John's naming ceremony about the name 'John' for they said nobody in the family ever bore that name.

67. Anna was an indigene of Asher, daughter of Phanuel and a prophetess

68. Addi is one of the ancestors of Jesus Christ.

69. The Greek name 'Addi' means my witness or my adorned.

70. Even 'sinners' unbelievers love those who love them

71. The woman's twelve years bleeding stopped when she touched the edge of Jesus' cloak.

72. Foxes have holes and birds of the air have nests, similarly the Son of Man also has his mansion to lay his head.

73. Jesus Christ taught the Lord's prayer on request.

74. Believers in Christ are advised to make efforts and enter through the narrow door because many will try to enter but in vain.

75. The elder brother of the prodigal son was happy at the party thrown to welcome the prodigal son.

76. Dogs licked the sores of poor Lazarus at the rich man's gate.

77. Those sent by Jesus Christ to untie the colt in the city found it just as he had told them.

78. At one time, the Pharisees advised Jesus Christ to rebuke his disciples but he replied "If they keep quiet, the stones will cry out."

79. Jesus Christ's first miracle was performed at Cana in Galilee.

80. Jesus Christ healed the royal officer's son from afar.

81. Jesus Christ says no one can come to Him unless the Father enables him.

82. The Sanhendrin conspired to kill Jesus Christ for two reasons:

     i. Fear of his spreading fame

     ii. That the Romans will take away their temple and nation

83. Akeldama means field of blood which belonged to Judas Iscariot.

84. While Paul and Silas were going to the place of prayer, they met the girl who had a spirit by which she predicted the future.

85. Jesus Christ is the foundation already laid which Christians are supposed to build on.

86. If a Christian has dispute with another Christian, they are to settle it in court.

87. Sexual immorality is sin committed against one's own body that is the temple of God.

88. Believers are ambassadors for Christ here on earth.

89. Since we are in this world, our battle is against flesh and blood.

90. The book of Revelation records that there was war in heaven when angel Michael and his angels fought against the dragon while the later and his angels fought back.

91. Jesus Christ was humble and obedient to even death on the cross.

92. In the last times there will be scoffers who will follow their own ungodly desires.

93. Archippus was advised to complete the work he received in the Lord.

94. The church in Smyrna was known to be in affliction and poverty yet rich.

95. Christians should pray only when there is persecution.

96. Apostle John reported that for sake of the 'Name', they went out and even received

help from the pagans.

97. Godliness without contentment can be great gain to Christians.

98. Obedience to the Word makes complete God's love in a Christian.

99. Believers are supposed to crave for pure spiritual milk so they can grow in their salvation.

100. According to Apostle Paul, the greatest among faith, hope and love is faith.

Chapter THREE CONTEXT QUESTIONS

In this chapter, questions aim at making the reader distinguish the particular text from other similar texts in the Holy Bible. They deal with only the text through being specific, clear and none other. Questions therefore touch on time, place who why when where and how among others. This knowledge will help the reader identify and distinguish scripture quotations by Satan that are out of context and only aimed at their spiritual downfall Knowing this will help them resist him as he flees.

.

The questions following have their answers within the text and the reader is to supply these answers.

1. "Young men, in the same way be submissive to those who are older. All of you clothe yourselves with humility toward one another, because 'God opposes the proud but gives grace to the humble' ".

   a. Who recorded this?———————————————————————————
   b. Who was addressed initially?———————————————————————
   c. Why was this statement made?——————————————————————
   d. Where can it be found in the Holy Bible?——————————————————

1. "These men are springs without water and mists driven by a storm. Blackest darkness is reserved for them".

   a. Who recorded this?———————————————————————————
   b. Who was addressed initially?———————————————————————
   c. Where can it be found in the Holy Bible?———————————————————

1. "If any of you lacks wisdom, he should ask God, who gives generously to all without finding fault, and it will be given to him".

a. Who spoke?——————————————————————————————————

b. To whom did he speak?————————————————————————————

c. Where is this statement found in the Holy Bible?————————————————————————

1. "But I did not want to do anything without your consent so that any favor you do will be spontaneous and not forced".

a. Who made this statement?————————————————————————

b. To whom and concerning who?————————————————————

c. Where is it found in the Holy Bible?——————————————————————

1. "At my defense, no one came to my support, but everyone deserted me. May it not be held against them"

a. Who made this statement?————————————————————————

b. To whom?——————————————————————————————

c. Where in the Holy Bible is this statement found?————————————————

1. "When you ask, you do not receive because you ask with wrong motives, that you may spend what you get on your pleasures".

a. Who recorded this statement?————————————————————————

b. To whom?————————————————————————————

c. Where in the Holy Bible is it found?————————————————————————————

1. "May the Lord show mercy to the household of Onesiphorus, because he often refreshed me and was not ashamed of my chains"

a. Who spoke?————————————————————————————

b. To whom?————————————————————————————

c. Where is the statement found in the Holy Bible?————————————————————————————

1. "Likewise, teach the older women to be reverent in the way they live, not to be slanderers or addicted to much wine, but to teach what is good".

a. Who recorded this statement?————————————————————————————

b. To whom was the statement made?————————————————————————————

c. Where is it found in the Holy Bible?————————————————————————————

1. "Confident of your obedience, I write to you, knowing that you will do even more than I ask. And one thing more: prepare a guest room for me, because I hope to be restored to you in answer to your prayers".

a. Who wrote this

letter?————————————————————————————

b. To whom did he write?————————————————————————

c. From where did he write?————————————————————————

d. Where is it found in the Holy Bible?———————————————————

1. "Remind the people to be subject to rulers and authorities, to be obedient, to be ready to do whatever is good"

a. Who made this statement?—————————————————————————.

b. To whom?——————————————————————————————

c. Which people are referred to here?—————————————————————·

d. Where in the Holy Bible is it found?————————————————————

1. "Be very careful, then, how you live – not as unwise but wise".

a. Who recorded this statement?——————————————————————

b. To whom?——————————————————————————————

c. Where is it found in the Holy Bible?————————————————————

1. "I know what it is to be in need, and I know what it is to be in plenty. I have learned the secret of being content in any and every situation, whether well fed or hungry, whether living in plenty or in want".

a. Who recorded this statement?———————————————————————

b. To whom?———————————————————————

c. On what occasion was the statement recorded?———————————————————————

d. Where in the Holy Bible is it found?———————————————————————

1. "But godliness with contentment is great gain".

a. Who recorded this statement?———————————————————————

b. To whom?———————————————————————

c. At what occasion?———————————————————————

d. Where is it found in the Holy Bible?———————————————————————

1. "For this reason God sends them a powerful delusion so that they will believe the lie".

a. Who spoke?———————————————————————

b. To whom?———————————————————————

c. On what occasion?———————————————————————

d. Where is it found in the Holy Bible?———————————————————————

1. "Devout yourselves to prayer being watchful and thankful".

a. Who made this statement?———————————————————————————————

b. To whom?———————————————————————————————

c. Where is it found in the Holy Bible?———————————————————————————————

1. "Therefore keep watch because you do not know the day or the hour".

a. Who spoke?———————————————————————————————

b. Where in the Holy Bible is this found?———————————————————————————————

1. "Wives submit to your husbands as to the Lord. Husbands love your wives, just as Christ loved the church and gave himself up for her".

a. Who recorded this statement?———————————————————————————————

b. Who were the initial recipients of this message?———————————————————————————————

c. Where in the Holy Bible is this found?———————————————————————————————

1. "But you, brothers are not in darkness so that this day should surprise you like a thief".

a. Who recorded this statement?———————————————————————————————

b. To whom?———————————————————————————————

  c. What day is referred to here?—————————————————————

  d. Where in the Holy Bible is it found?—————————————————————

1. "For he has rescued us from the dominion of darkness and brought us into the kingdom of the Son he loves".

  a. Who spoke?—————————————————————

  b. Who is addressed?—————————————————————

  c. Who did the rescue?—————————————————————

  d. Where in the Holy Bible is it found?—————————————————————

1. "For even when we were with you, we gave you this rule, 'If a man will not work, he shall not eat' ".

  a. Who recorded this?—————————————————————

  b. Who is the initial recipient?—————————————————————

  c. On what occasion was this statement made?—————————————————————

  d. Where in the Holy Bible is it found?—————————————————————

1. "That day Herod and Pilate became friends – before this they had been enemies".

  a. On what occasion did this take

place?———————————————————————

b. Where in the Holy Bible is it found?————————————————————

1. "Teacher, I beg you to look at my son, for he is my only child. A spirit seizes him and he suddenly screams; it throws him into convulsion so that he foams at the mouth - - - could not".

a. Who made this statement?————————————————————————

b. To whom?————————————————————————

c. What did the disciples do?————————————————————————

d. Where in the Holy Bible is this found?————————————————————

1. "I press on toward the goal to win the prize for which God has called me heavenward in Christ Jesus".

a. Who made this statement?————————————————————————

b. To whom?————————————————————————

c. Where in the Holy Bible is it found?————————————————————

1. "Now leave him alone, Let's see if Elijah comes to save him".

a. Who is referred to in this statement?————————————————————

b. When and where did this take place?————————————————————

c. Where in the Holy Bible is this found?——————————————————————————————·

1. "... As apostles of Christ we could have been a burden to you ..."

a. Who made this statement?—————————————————————————————

b. To whom?——————————————————————————·

c. On what occasion?——————————————————————————·

d. Where in the Holy Bible is it found?——————————————————————————·

1. "When the islanders saw the snake hanging from his hand, they said to each other, 'This man must be a murderer; for though he escaped from the sea, justice has not allowed him to live' ".

a. Who is referred to in this statement?—————————————————————————

b. What Island was it?—————————————————————————

c. What happened to the snake?—————————————————————————

d. Where was he travelling to?—————————————————————————

1. "For it is by grace you have been saved, through faith – and this not from yourselves, it is the gift of God – not by works, so that no one can boast".

a. Who was inspired by the Holy spirit to make this statement?————————————————

b. Who was the initial recipient?——————————————————————

c. Where in the Holy Bible is it found?—————————————————————

1. "Behold, I am coming soon! My reward is with me, and I will give to everyone according to what he has done . . ."

a. Who is speaking here?—————————————————————————-

b. Where in the Holy Bible is it found?————————————————————

1. "Rabbi, who sinned, this man or his parents, that he was born blind?"

a. Who asked this question?————————————————————————

b. What was Jesus' response?—————————————————————————

c. What did Jesus later do?—————————————————————————

d. Where in the Holy Bible is this found?————————————————————

1. "The scripture foresaw that God would justify the Gentiles by faith, and announced the gospel in advance to Abraham; 'All nations will be blessed through you". So those who have faith are blessed along with Abraham, the man of faith' ".

a. Who recorded this

statement?——————————————————————————

b. Where in the Holy Bible is it found?——————————————————————————

1. "I gave you milk, not solid food, for you were not yet ready for it. Indeed you are still not ready".

a. Who made this statement?——————————————————————————

b. Who is addressed here?——————————————————————————

c. On what occasion?——————————————————————————

d. Where in the Holy Bible is it found?——————————————————————————

1. "Do not be deceived: God cannot be mocked. A man reaps what he sows".

a. Who recorded this statement?——————————————————————————

b. Where in the Holy Bible is it found?——————————————————————————

1. "Brothers, my heart's desire and prayer to God for the Israelites is that they may be saved".

a. Who made this statement?——————————————————————————

b. Who were the initial recipients of this message?——————————————————————————

c. Where in the Holy Bible is this found?——————————————————————————

1. "Because you are sons, God has sent the Spirit of his Son into our hearts, the Spirit who calls out 'Abba Father' ".

   a. Who recorded this statement?———————————————————————————

   b. Who were initially addressed?———————————————————————————.

   c. Where in the Holy Bible is it found?———————————————————————————

1. "That if you confess with your mouth "Jesus is Lord" and believe in your heart that God raised him from the dead, you will be saved".

   a. Who was addressed initially?———————————————————————————

   b. Where in the Holy Bible is it found?———————————————————————————

1. "But the fruit of the Spirit is love, joy, peace, patience, kindness, goodness, faithfulness, gentleness and self-control. Against such things, there is no law".

   a. What can be contrasted with the fruit of the Spirit in this context?———————————————

   b. On what occasion was this said?———————————————————————————

   c. Where in the Holy Bible is this found?———————————————————————————

1. "And how can they preach unless they are sent? As it is written, 'How beautiful are the feet of those who bring good news!' "

a. What gave rise to this statement?————————————————————————

b. Who made the statement?————————————————————————

c. Where in the Holy Bible is it found?————————————————————

1. "Examine yourselves to see whether you are in the faith; test yourselves. Do you not realize that Christ Jesus is in you – unless, of course, you fail the test?"

a. At what stage of the writer's correspondence did he make this statement?————————————————————————

b. Who are the initial recipients?————————————————————————

c. Where in the Holy Bible is it found?————————————————————

1. "For the wages of sin is death, but the gift of God is eternal life in Christ Jesus our Lord".

a. Who recorded this statement?————————————————————————

b. To whom?————————————————————————

c. Where in the Holy Bible is it found?————————————————————

1. "For such men are false apostles, deceitful workmen, masquerading as apostles of Christ".

a. On what occasion was this statement made?————————————————————————

b. Who made the statement?———————————————————————————

c. Where in the Holy Bible is it found?———————————————————————

1. "Therefore, my brothers, be eager to prophesy, and do not forbid speaking in tongues. But everything should be done in a fitting and orderly way".

a. Who made this statement?———————————————————————————

b. On what occasion was this statement made?———————————————————————

c. Where in the Holy Bible is it found?———————————————————————

1. "Now finish the work, so that your willingness to do it may be matched by your completion of it, according to your means".

a. Who made this statement?———————————————————————————

b. To whom?———————————————————————————

c. What occasion?———————————————————————————

d. Where in the Holy Bible is it found?———————————————————————

1. "For all have sinned and fall short of the glory of God".

a. Who are the initial recipients of this message?———————————————————————

b. Where in the Holy Bible is this

found?——————————————————————————.

1. "You show that you are a letter from Christ, the result of our ministry, written not with ink but with the Spirit of the living God, not on tablets of stone but on tablets of human hearts".

a. Who recorded this statement?—————————————————————————

b. To whom?————————————————————————.

c. Where in the Holy Bible is this found?————————————————————————

1. "Can both fresh water and salt water flow from the same spring?"

a. Who recorded this statement?—————————————————————————

b. On what occasion?————————————————————————.

c. Where in the Holy Bible is it found?————————————————————————.

1. "Salvation is found in no one else, for there is no other name under heaven given to men by which we must be saved".

a. Who made this statement?—————————————————————————

b. On what occasion?————————————————————————.

c. Where in the Holy Bible is it found?————————————————————————.

1. "A person who has had a bath needs only to wash his feet; his whole body is clean. And you are clean though not everyone of you".

   a. Who made this statement?—————————————————————————

   b. To whom?—————————————————————————————

   c. On what occasion?————————————————————————————

   d. Where in the Holy Bible is it found?——————————————————————

1. "This is what I told you while I was still with you. Everything must be fulfilled that is written about me in the law of Moses, the Prophets and the Psalms".

   a. Who spoke?————————————————————————————————

   b. To whom?—————————————————————————————————

   c. On what occasion?————————————————————————————

   d. Where in the Holy Bible is this found?——————————————————————

1. "But Christ has indeed been raised from the dead, the first fruits of those who have fallen asleep".

   a. Who made this statement?—————————————————————————

   b. Where in the Holy Bible is this found?——————————————————————

1. "The one I kiss is the man; arrest him and lead him away under guard".

a. Who spoke?————————————————————————

b. To whom?————————————————————————

c. About whom did he speak?————————————————————————

d. What occasion?————————————————————————

e. Where in the Holy Bible is it found?————————————————————————

1. "And my God will meet all your needs according to his glorious riches in Christ Jesus".

a. Who made this statement?————————————————————————

b. On what occasion?————————————————————————

c. Where in the Holy Bible is this found?————————————————————————

1. "I thank Christ Jesus our Lord, who has given me strength, that he considered me faithful, appointing me to his service".

a. Who made this statement?————————————————————————

b. To whom?————————————————————————

c. Where in the Holy Bible is this found?————————————————————————

1. "Watch and pray so that you will not fall into temptation. The spirit is willing but the body is weak".

   a. Who spoke?————————————————————————————
   b. To who?————————————————————————————
   c. Where?————————————————————————————
   d. When?————————————————————————————
   e. Where in the Holy Bible is this found?————————————————————————————

1. "For our struggle is not against flesh and blood, but against the rulers, against the authorities, against the powers of this dark world and against the spiritual forces of evil in the heavenly realms".

   a. Who made this statement?————————————————————————————
   b. Who are the initial recipients of this statement?————————————————————————————
   c. Where in the Holy Bible is this found?————————————————————————————

1. "No one sews a patch of unshrunk cloth on an old garment. If he does, the new piece will pull away from the old, making the tear worse."

   a. Who spoke?————————————————————————————
   b. To whom?————————————————————————————
   c. On what

occasion?———————————————————————————

d. When   in   the   Holy   Bible   is   this found?————————————————————————————

1. "Whatever happens, conduct yourselves in a manner worthy of the gospel of Christ. Then whether I come and see you or only hear about you in my absence, I will know that you stand firm in one spirit, contending as one man for the faith of the gospel without being frightened in any way by those who oppose you . . . and that by God".

a. Who   made   this statement?———————————————————————

b. To whom?————————————————————————————

c. Where   in   the   Holy   Bible   is   this found?————————————————————————————

1. "You are worried and upset about many things, but one thing is needed . . . and it will not be taken away from her".

a. Who   made   this speech?—————————————————————————

b. To whom?————————————————————————————

c. Why?————————————————————————————

d. Where   in   the   Holy   Bible   is   it found?————————————————————————————

1. "Now at the feast the Jews were watching for him and asking, "Where is that man?"

a. What

feast?—————————————————————————.

b. Who is the man they sought?—————————————————————-

c. What did he do halfway through the feast?—————————————————.

d. What were some three major reactions of these Jews?—————————————————

e. Where in the Holy Bible is this found?—————————————————————

1. "For since the creation of the world God's invisible qualities – his eternal power and divine nature – have been closely seen, being understood from what has been made so that men are without excuse".

a. Who made this statement?—————————————————————

b. To whom?—————————————————————————

c. Where the Holy Bible is it found?—————————————————————

1. "In fact, the law requires that nearly everything be cleansed with blood, and without the shedding of blood there is no forgiveness".

a. What has the blood done for man?————————————————————.

b. Where in the Holy Bible is this found?—————————————————————

1. "The kingdom of heaven is like yeast that a woman took and mixed into a large amount of flour until it worked all through

the dough".

a. Who
    spoke?————————————————————————————————————
b. What   part   of   speech   is   used
    here?————————————————————————————————————
c. Where   in   the   Holy   Bible   is   this
    found?————————————————————————————————————.

1. "Throw your net on the right side of the boat and you will find
    some"

a. Who
    spoke?————————————————————————————————————
b. To
    whom?————————————————————————————————————
c. On   what
    occasion?————————————————————————————————————
d. Where   in   the   Holy   Bible   is   this
    found?————————————————————————————————————

1. "Whatever town or village you enter, search for some worthy
    person there and stay at his house until you leave".

a. Who   gave   this
    instruction?————————————————————————————————————
b. To
    whom?————————————————————————————————————
c. On   what
    occasion?————————————————————————————————————
d. Where   in   the   Holy   Bible   is   this
    found?————————————————————————————————————

1. "Brothers and fathers, listen now to my defense".

   a. Who spoke?————————————————————————

   b. On what occasion?————————————————————

   c. What was the crowd's initial reaction?————————————————

   d. Where in the Holy Bible is it found?————————————————

1. "Nevertheless, I have this against you: You tolerate that woman Jezebel, who calls herself a prophetess. By her teaching, she misleads my servants into sexual immorality and the eating of food sacrificed to idols".

   a. Who is addressed?————————————————————————.

   b. Who spoke?————————————————————————

   c. Where in the Holy Bible is this found?————————————

1. "But there are some Jews from the province of Asia, who ought to be here before you and bring charges if they have anything against me".

   a. Who made this statement?————————————————————.

   b. On what occasion?————————————————————

   c. Who was interrogating him?————————————————————

d. Where in the Holy Bible is this found?———————————————————————

1. "But whatever was my profit I now consider loss for the sake of Christ".

a. Who made this statement?———————————————————————
b. To whom?———————————————————————
c. Where in the Holy Bible is this found?———————————————————————

1. "But they remained silent. So taking hold of the man, he healed him and sent him away".

a. Who was healed———————————————————————
b. Who are they that remained silent?———————————————————————
c. Where did this take place?———————————————————————
d. When did this occur?———————————————————————
e. Where in the Holy Bible is this found?———————————————————————

1. "I have much to write to you, but I do not want to use paper and ink. Instead, I hope to visit you and talk with you face to face so that our joy may be complete".

a. Who made this statement?———————————————————————

b. To whom?———————————————————————

c. Where in the Holy Bible is this found?———————————————————————

1. "Yet I hold this against you: You have forsaken your first love".

a. Who was addressed?———————————————————————·

b. What however did she have in her credit?———————————————————————

c. Where in the Holy Bible is this found?———————————————————————

1. "I write these things to you who believe in the name of the Son of God so that you may know that you have eternal life".

a. What does this verse give the believer?———————————————————————

b. Who recorded the speech?———————————————————————

c. Where in the Holy Bible is this found?———————————————————————

1. "'- - - Let both grow together until the harvest. At that time I will tell the harvesters: First collect the weeds and tie them in bundles to be burned; then gather the wheat and bring it into my barn'".

a. Who spoke?———————————————————————

b. On what occasion?———————————————————————

c. Where in the Holy Bible is this found?————————————————————————————

1. "I know your deeds, that you are neither cold nor hot. I wish you were either one or the other!"

a. Who is addressed?————————————————————————————

b. Who spoke?————————————————————————————

c. Where in the Holy Bible is this found?————————————————————————————

1. "Even though my illness was a trial to you, you did not treat me with contempt or scorn. Instead you welcomed me as if I were an angel of God or as if I were Christ Jesus himself"

a. Who made this statement?————————————————————————————

b. To whom?————————————————————————————

c. What was the illness?————————————————————————————

d. Where in the Holy Bible is it found?————————————————————————————

1. "In the very same way, these dreamers pollute their own bodies, reject authority and slander celestial beings".

a. Who recorded this statement?————————————————————————————

b. Who are referred to here?————————————————————————————

c. Where in the Holy Bible is this found?———————————————————————————

1. "Your prayers and gifts to the poor have come up as a memorial offering before God . . ."

a. Whose prayer?———————————————————————————
b. Who gave this answer?———————————————————————————.
c. What did he (the man that prayed) do after this answer?———————————————————————————.
d. Where in the Holy bible is this found?———————————————————————————

1. "If it is the Lord's will, we will live and do this or that".

a. Who recorded this statement?———————————————————————————
b. On what occasion?———————————————————————————
c. Where in the Holy Bible is this found?———————————————————————————

1. "This sickness will not end in death. No it is for God's glory so that God's Son may be gloried through it."

a. Who spoke?———————————————————————————
b. Whose sickness was it?———————————————————————————.
c. How was God's name glorified?———————————————————————————

d. Where in the Holy Bible is this found?————————————————————————

1. "Hypocrites! You know how to interpret the appearance of the earth and the sky. How is it that you don't know how to interpret this present time?"

a. Who spoke?————————————————————————
b. To whom?————————————————————————
c. Where in the Holy Bible is this found?————————————————————————

1. "Dear friend, do not imitate what is evil but what is good. Anyone who does what is good is from God. Anyone who does what is evil has not seen God".

a. Who recorded this statement?————————————————————————
b. Who was initially addressed?————————————————————————
c. Where in the Holy Bible is it found?————————————————————————

Chapter FOUR DIRECT QUESTIONS

Questions in this chapter seek to know the what, who when where and how. They also trace, list explain and state about people and events in the Holy Bible. The reader needs to take time and think meditatively before supplying the answers

.

1. Where did Jesus Christ appear to his disciples forty days after his resurrection?————————————————————————————————————.

2. Where and on what day of the week did Jesus' crucifixion and death take place?——————————————————————————————————

3. Where did Jesus quieted the storm?——————————————————————————————————

4. In which town did a sinful woman anoint Jesus Christ's feet?——————————————————————-

5. Where did Jesus Christ choose his disciples?——————————————————————————————————

6. Who baptized Jesus Christ and where did the event take place?——————————————————————————————————

7. On what sea did Jesus Christ appear to his disciples while they were fishing?——————————————————————————————————

8. Into which city did Jesus Christ triumphantly enter?————————————————————————————————-

9. Where did Jesus Christ feed five thousand people?——————————————————————————————————

10. Where did Jesus Christ curse the fig tree?——————————————————————————————————

11. Why did Apostle Paul leave Titus in

Crete?——————————————————————————————————-

12. According to the Holy Bible, how are husbands to love their wives?———————————————————————————

13. Who led the Ethiopian eunuch (pilgrim) to Christ?—————————————————————————

14. Can a believer love both God and the world at the same time?————————————————-

15. Since the earth and all in it shall be destroyed what kind of life are Christians expected to live?——————————————————-

16. How can salvation be obtained?————————————————————

17. Which is the first commandment with a promise?———————————————————

18. Where did Jesus Christ attend the Feast of Tabernacle?——————————————————————-

19. What are the qualifications of a deacon?————————————————————

20. What was Jesus Christ's second miracle and where was it performed?————————————————————

21. At what age and condition does a widow qualify to be enlisted by the church?——————————————————

22. Does God tempt his children?———————————————————

23. In his upbringing, who taught Timothy?———————————————————

24. What did Ruth later become to Jesus Christ?——————————————————

25. What does Truth do for the believer?———————————————————

26. Through whose witness did Timothy get

converted?——————————————————————————

27. What does meditation accomplish in the life of a believer?———————————————————————

28. According to what does God promise to meet believers' needs?——————————————————————

29. On what tree did Zacchaeus climb to see Jesus Christ?——————————————————————

30. Besides listening to the word of God, what should the believer also do?——————————————————————————

31. Though brought up with the knowledge of the Holy Scriptures (II Timothy 3:15), why was Timothy not circumcised until when he met Paul?——————————————————————

32. Whose baby leaped in the womb on its mother being greeted and who brought the greetings?——————————————————————

33. Of what importance is yeast in the Holy Bible with regards to the kingdom of God?——————————————————————

34. Besides the answer in '33' above, what other things does yeast symbolize?——————————————————————

35. Will there be use of songs and musical instruments when Christ returns?——————————————————————

36. How many biographical books are there in the New Testament, name them in their order?——————————————————————

37. Why do communicant members take the Lord's Supper?——————————————————————

38. Mark deserted Apostle Paul in Pamphylia, when did he join Paul again as a fellow

worker?————————————————————————

39. What should be the believer's response to God for being set free?

40. How many of Jesus' disciples were fishermen before they were called, name them?————————————————————————

41. How many historical books are there in the New Testament, name them?————————————————————————

42. Which books are prophetic in the New Testament, name them?————————————————————————

43. On what day of the week did Jesus Christ heal the crippled woman?————————————————————————

44. Why was King Herod pleased to see Jesus Christ?————————————————————————

45. List the Epistles written by Apostle Paul in their order as seen in the New Testament?————————————————————————

46. List the general Epistles in their order as seen in the New Testament?————————————————————————

47. Through what occasion or incidence did Kings Pilate and Herod become friends?————————————————————————

48. What did Jesus Christ say is his food?————————————————————————

49. Cephas and Peter are the same name – meaning 'Rock', in what languages respectively?————————————————————————

50. What did Simeon say after he saw and held the baby Jesus in his arms?————————————————————————

51. With what question did Nicodemus confront Jesus

Christ?——————————————————————————

52. What did Mary, mother of Jesus Christ and Joseph her husband go to Jerusalem for every year?——————————————————————————

53. How did healing take place at the pool and at what frequency?——————————————————————————

54. Did Jesus' disciples heal the possessed boy brought by his father?————————————————

55. What day of the week did Jesus Christ heal the sick man at the pool of Bethesda?——————————————————————————

56. What language is 'lying' to the Devil?——————————————————————————

57. What was the secret of the rich generosity of the Macedonian Churches?——————————————————————————·

58. What was Apostles Paul's prayer for the Macedonian Churches?——————————————————————————·

59. a. Why didn't the centurion go with his servant to Jesus Christ but rather

sent that Jesus should come?——————————————————————————·

b. Why did the Jews support his act?——————————————————————————·

1. Why should the immoral brother (according to Apostle Paul), be handed over to Satan (expelled) from the congregation?——————————————————————————

2. What are some ingredients of saints' fellowship that resulted in what is known today as the church?——————————————————————————

3. What does taking the Lord's Supper unworthily result

into?——————————————————————————————

4. Why did the soldiers plan to kill all the prisoners on board with them (including Apostle Paul) to Rome?——————————————————————————————.

5. Is it possible for someone without the Holy Spirit belong to Christ?————————————————

6. Due to God's abundant grace, shall man continue in sin?————————————————————————·

7. What was the outcome of Apostle Paul's first letter to the church at Corinth?——————————————————————————————

8. On what account was Apostle Paul considered a god by his fellow crew men on the Island of Malta?——————————————————————————————

9. On which day of the week was Jesus Christ crucified?——————————————————————————·

10. How did Paul and Barnabas react to the intended sacrifice by the people of Lystra to them as gods?——————————————————————————————

11. After preaching in the synagogue at Nazareth, how did Jesus Christ escape being killed by the people (his audience)?——————————————————————————————

12. On what day of the week did Jesus Christ heal the man with dropsy?——————————————————————————————

13. King Agrippa was convinced that Apostle Paul was not insane. What therefore prevented him from releasing him?——————————————————————————————

14. What was the people's immediate reaction when Paul and Barnabas healed the cripple in Lystra?——————————————————————————————.

15. Where did Peter and John heal the man who was lame from birth?——————————————————————————————

16. What assured the women who went to Jesus' tomb, of His resurrection?—————————————————————————————.

17. What action led to the conversion of the proconsul, Sergius Paulus?—————————————————————————————

18. What miraculous things took place shortly before Jesus' crucifixion?—————————————————————————————

19. Which Church in the book of Revelation did God say 'I have placed before you an open door that no one can shut'?—————————————————————————————

20. What was the desire of those who planned to arrest and have Stephen killed?—————————————————————————————

21. Why is God patient with man?—————————————————————————————

22. In which town was Jesus Christ born?—————————————————————————————.

23. On his crucifixion, what two things happened to the bloodshed by Christ?—————————————————————————————

24. What unique quality were the believers in Berea known for?—————————————————————————————

25. What significant thing did Herod do in Bethlehem after he knew of Jesus' birth through the Magi?—————————————————————————————

26. According to Apostle Paul, what are some things that true circumcision involve?—————————————————————————————.

27. When and where was Jesus Christ baptized with the Holy Spirit?—————————————————————————————

28. According to the book of James in the Holy Bible, what are believers not expected to do as image bearers of God?—————————————————————————————.

29. Why did all the widows in town cry when Dorcas died?————————————————————————

30. Who appointed elders in the early church?————————————————————————

31. a. What was Herod's plan against the boy Jesus?————————————————————————

b. Who revealed Herod's plan to Jesus' earthly parents and how?————————————————————————

c. What did Joseph and Mary do?————————————————————————

1. After Paul's repentance, the disciples were still afraid of him. Who brought him to them and explained satisfactorily his new status?————————————————————————

2. Who is that disciple that died and was raised by Peter in Joppa?————————————————————————

3. When the Thessalonians Jews learned that Paul was in Berea, what did they do?————————————————————————

4. What are some characteristics of Christian baptism?————————————————————————

5. As recorded in Paul's Epistle to the Galatian church, why did he (Paul) oppose Peter?————————————————————————

6. From where and how did Jesus Christ get money to pay tax for himself and Peter?————————————————————————

7. How does the Holy Bible in the books of Luke and Ephesians tell believers to treat their neighbors?————————————————————————

8. According to the book of Acts in the Holy Bible, Galileo was proconsul of Achaia when the Jews united and made an attack on Paul, bringing him for judgment. Why did the proconsul refuse to judge the case?————————————————————————————

9. According to Revelation 16:21, why did men curse God?————————————————————————————.

10. Who brought Stephen before the assembly where subsequently he was killed?————————————————————————————

CHAPTER FIVE AT LEAST FOUR CHARACTERISTICS EACH OF IDENTIFIED PERSONS

Certain characteristics of some persons in the Holy Bible are similar, just as the times they lived and acted may seem confusing. This chapter lists names of some persons and it is intended for the reader to get more composed as they think through in order to clearly supply at least four characteristics of each.

1. Titus
2. Philip (one of the seven deacons)
3. Anna
4. Abel
5. Aristobulus
6. Annas
7. Herodias
8. Martha
9. Zacchaeus
10. Timothy: His life as co-worker with Paul
11. Persis
12. Abraham: Significance in the New Testament
13. Nicodemus
14. Zechariah: Father of John the Baptist
15. Andronicus
16. Simeon
17. Tryphena
18. Gaius of Corinth
19. Agabus
20. Gabriel
21. Philip: Disciple of Jesus Christ. Matthew 10:3; Mark 3:18

22. Matthew
23. Epenetus
24. Andrew
25. Elizabeth
26. Herod Agrippa 1
27. Junais
28. Cain
29. Ampliatus
30. Elijah
31. Paul: Background
32. Stephen
33. Urbanus
34. Silas
35. Caiaphas
36. Matthias
37. Demetrius
38. Apelles
39. Bartholomew
40. Dorcas (Tabitha)
41. David
42. Stachys
43. Cornelius
44. Barabbas
45. Apollos
46. Festus
47. Herodion
48. Felix
49. Aquila
50. Joseph: Husband of Mary, Mother of Jesus Christ.
51. Lydia
52. Simon: The tanner
53. Ananias: Husband of Sapphira

54. Thomas (Didymus)
55. Narcissus
56. Agrippa
57. Esau
58. Jairus
59. Asyncritus
60. Herod Antipas
61. Priscilla
62. Ananias: Disciple in Damascus
63. Phlegon
64. Tertius
65. Barnabas
66. Isaac
67. Salome
68. Peter: Character and significance as one of the major leaders of the church.
69. Jacob: Significance in the New Testament
70. Rufus
71. Erastus
72. John the Baptist
73. Jason
74. Ananias: A high priest
75. Tryphosa
76. Patrobas
77. Hermas
78. John: Disciple of Jesus; Events after Jesus' ascension
79. Moses
80. Mary: Mother of Jesus
81. Pilate
82. Philologus
83. Mary: Sister of Martha and Lazarus
84. Joseph: The rich man from Arimathea

Chapter SIX
RECITATION OF CONTENT

This chapter has similarities with the chapter on fill in the gaps. Certain verse(s) from the Holy Bible are written without omission of any part. It is intended to help the reader learn and know the scripture by heart in order to use it as a weapon in spiritual warfare, the same way Jesus Christ did in defeating Satan, as recorded in Matthew 4:1-11and Luke 4: 3-12

It will help the reader know that the enemy quotes scripture to believers mainly to cause them fall into sin. Knowing and applying scripture will therefore help one stand at such times as Jesus Christ did. The reader is expected to tell the source - book, chapter and verse(s).

1. "Do not conform any longer to the pattern of this world, but be transformed by the renewing of your mind. Then you will be able to test and approve what God's will is – his good, pleasing and perfect will".

1. "First of all, you must understand that in the last days scoffers will come, scoffing and following their own evil desires".

1. "Then all the virgins woke up and trimmed their lamps".

1. "Do not lie to each other, since you have taken off your old self with its practices".

1. "Remember your leaders, who spoke the word of God to you. Consider the outcome of their way of life and imitate their faith".

1. "But the cowardly, the unbelieving, the vile, the murderers, the

sexually immoral, those who practice magic arts, the idolaters and all liars – their place will be in the fiery lake of burning sulfur. This is the second death".

1. "So, if you think you are standing firm, be careful that you don't fall".

1. "Jesus said to her, 'Mary'. She turned toward him and cried out in Aramaic, 'Rabboni!' (which means teacher)".

1. "Woe to them! They have taken the way of Cain; they have rushed for profit into Balaam's error; they have been destroyed in Korah's rebellion".

1. "For the Son of Man came to seek and to save what was lost".

1. "Be imitators of God, therefore, as dearly loved children".
2. "In the same way, faith by itself, if it is not accompanied by action, is dead".

1. "We demolish arguments and every pretension that sets itself up against the knowledge of God, and we take captive every thought to make it obedient to Christ".

1. "Now the Bereans were of more noble character than the Thessalonians, for they received the message with great eagerness and examined the scriptures everyday to see if what Paul said was true".

1. "A third angel followed them and said in a loud voice: "If anyone worships the beast and his image and receives his mark on the forehead or on the hand, he, too, will drink of the wine of God's fury which has been poured full strength into the cup

of his wrath. He will be tormented with burning sulfur in the presence of the holy angels and of the Lamb".

1. "I have been crucified with Christ and I no longer live, but Christ lives in me. The life I live in the body, I live by faith in the Son of God, who loved me and gave himself for me".

1. " 'Put your sword back in its place,' Jesus said to him, 'for all who draw the sword will die by the sword".

1. "What shall we say, then? Shall we go on sinning so that grace may increase? By no means! We died to sin; how can we live in it any longer?"

1. "Each of the four living creatures had six wings and was covered with eyes all around, even under his wings Day and night they never stop saying:

'Holy, holy, holy
is the Lord God Almighty.
Who was, and is, and is to come' ".

1. "If they fall away, to be brought back to repentance, because to their loss they are crucifying the Son of God all over again and subjecting him to public disgrace".

1. "Who, being in very nature God, did not consider equality with God something to be grasped".

1. "Be very careful then, how you live – not as unwise but as wise"

1. "Now get up and go into the city, and you will be told what

you must do."

2. "But mark this: There will be terrible times in the last days".

1. "If we confess our sins, he is faithful and just and will forgive us our sins and purify us from all unrighteousness".

1. "But you, dear friends, build yourselves up in your most holy faith and pray in the Holy Spirit".

1. "Do not be deceived: God cannot be mocked. A man reaps what he sows".

1. "Dear friend, I pray that you may enjoy good health and that all may go well with you, even as your soul is getting along well".

1. "Be joyful always; pray continually".

1. "Therefore, if anyone is in Christ, he is a new creation; the old has gone, the new has come!"

1. "If this is so, then the Lord knows how to rescue godly men from trials and to hold the unrighteous for the day of judgment, while continuing their punishment".

1. "Thus there were fourteen generations in all from Abraham to David, fourteen from David to the exile to Babylon, and fourteen from the exile to the Christ".

1. "Then I heard another voice from heaven say: 'Come out of her, my people, so that you will not share in her sins, so that you will not receive any of her plagues' "

1. "Anyone, then, who knows the good he ought to do and

doesn't do it, sins".

1. "Then you will know the truth and the truth will set you free".

1. "And these signs will accompany those who believe: In my name they will drive out demons: they will speak in new tongues"

1. "They called to the mountains and the rocks, 'Fall on us and hide us from the face of him who sits on the throne and from the wrath of the lamb'".

1. "I eagerly expect and hope that I will in no way be ashamed, but will have sufficient courage so that now as always Christ will be exalted in my body, whether by life or by death".

2. "And we know that in all things God works for the good of those who love him, who have been called according to his purpose".

1. "For this reason, since the day we heard about you, we have not stopped praying for you and asking God to fill you with the knowledge of his will through all spiritual wisdom and understanding".

1. "And pray that we may be delivered from wicked and evil men, for not everyone has faith".

1. "In the past God spoke to our forefathers through the prophets at many times and in various ways"

1. "I am coming soon. Hold on to what you have, so that no one will take your crown".

1. "But you will receive power when the Holy Spirit comes on you; and you will be my witnesses in Jerusalem, and in all Judea and Samaria, and to the ends of the earth".

1. "When he had led them out to the vicinity of Bethany, he lifted up his hands and blessed them. While he was blessing them, he left them and was taken up into heaven".

1. "You belong to your father, the devil, and you want to carry out your father's desire. He was a murderer from the beginning, not holding to the truth, for there is no truth in him. When he lies, he speaks his native language, for he is a liar and the father of lies".

1. "For it is by grace you have been saved, through faith – and this not from yourselves, it is the gift of God –not by works, so that no one can boast".

1. "So if I come, I will call attention to what he is doing, gossiping, maliciously about us. Not satisfied with that, he refuses to welcome the brothers. He also stops those who want to do so and puts them out of the church".

1. "For there are many rebellious people mere talkers and deceivers, especially those of the circumcision group. They must be silenced, because they are ruining whole households by teaching things they ought not to teach – and that for the sake of dishonest gain".

1. "There are different kinds of gifts, but the same Spirit".

1. "Cornelius answered: Four days ago I was in my house praying at this hour, at three in the afternoon. Suddenly a man in

shining clothes stood before me ".

2. "This title was written on her forehead:

MYSTERY

BABYLON THE GREAT

THE MOTHER OF PROSTITUTES

AND OF THE ABOMINATIONS OF THE EARTH"

1. "Jesus said to his disciples: 'Things that cause people to sin are bound to come, but woe o that person through whom they come' ".

1. "It would be better for him to be thrown into the sea with a millstone tied around his neck than for him to cause one of these little ones to sin".

1. "I pray that you may be active in sharing your faith, so that you will have a full understanding of every good thing we have in Christ".

1. "We ought therefore to show hospitality to such men so that we may work together for the truth".

1. "Tongues, then, are a sign not for believers but for unbelievers; prophecy, however, is for believers, not for unbelievers".

1. "After Herod died, an angel of the Lord appeared in a dream to Joseph in Egypt".

1. "They devoted themselves to the Apostles' teaching and to the fellowship, to the breaking of bread and to prayer".

1. "You must teach what is in accord with sound doctrine".

1. "If anyone has material possessions and sees his brother in
   need but has no pity on him, how can the love of God be in
   him".

1. "I want to know Christ and the power of his resurrection and
   the fellowship of sharing in his sufferings, becoming like him
   in his death".

1. "The thief comes only to steal and kill and destroy; I have
   come that they may have life, and have it to the full".

1. "Cast all your anxiety on him because he cares for you".

1. "For all have sinned and fall short of the glory of God".
2. "No, I beat my body and make it my slave so that after I have
   preached to others, I myself will not be disqualified for the
   prize".

1. "I looked, and there before me was a white horse! Its rider
   held a bow, and he was given a crown, and he rode out as a
   conqueror bent on conquest".

1. "Before certain men came from James, he used to eat with the
   Gentiles. But when they arrived, he began to draw back and
   separate himself from the Gentiles because he was afraid of
   those who belonged to the circumcision group".

1. "Then Philip ran up to the chariot and heard the man reading
   Isaiah the prophet. 'Do you understand what you are
   reading?' Philip asked".

1. "Here he is, speaking publicly, and they are not saying a word
   to him. Have the authorities really concluded that he is the

Christ?"

1. "So I tell you this, and insist on it in the Lord, that you must no longer live as the Gentiles do, in the futility of their thinking".

1. "Now may the Lord of peace himself give you peace at all times and in every way. The Lord be with all of you".

1. "Confident of your obedience I write to you, knowing that you will do even more than I ask".

1. "And this is love: that we walk in obedience to his commands. As you have heard from the beginning, his command is that you walk in love".

1. "Now faith is being sure of what we hope for and certain of what we do not see".

1. "And the peace of God, which transcends all understanding, will guard your hearts and your minds in Christ Jesus".

1. "Similarly, encourage the young men to be self-controlled".

1. "You yourselves are our letter, written on our hearts, known and read by everybody".

1. "Masters, provide your slaves with what is right and fair, because you know that you also have a Master in heaven".
2. "For God's gift and his call are irrevocable".
3. "Nevertheless, I have a few things against you: You have people there who hold to the teaching of Balaam, who taught Balak to entice the Israelites to sin by eating food sacrificed to

idols and by committing sexual immorality".

1. "The Spirit clearly says that in later times some will abandon the faith and follow deceiving spirits and things taught by demons".

1. "The Lord is not slow in keeping his promise, as some understand slowness. He is patient with you, not wanting anyone to perish, but everyone to come to repentance".

1. "For all have sinned and fall short of the glory of God".

1. "And anyone who does not carry his cross and follow me cannot be my disciple".

1. "Later the others also came, 'Sir! Sir!' they said 'Open the door for us!' "

1. "Do not rebuke an older man harshly but exhort him as if he were your father. Treat younger men as brothers".

1. "There remains, then, a Sabbath-rest for the people of God".

1. "Therefore dear friends, since you already know this, be on your guard so that you may not be carried away by the error of lawless men and fall from your secure position".

1. "Finally, be strong in the Lord and in his mighty power".

1. "And if Christ has not been raised, our preaching is useless and so is your faith".

1. "It has given me great joy to find some of your children walking in the truth, just as the Father commanded us".

1. "But only one thing is needed. Mary has chosen what is better, and it will not be taken away from her".

1. "For where two or three come together in my name, there am I with them".

1. "Be merciful to those who doubt".

1. "Let us fix our eyes on Jesus, the author and finisher of our faith, who for the joy set before him endured the cross, scorning its shame, and sat down at the right hand of the throne of God".

1. "Let your gentleness be evident to all. The Lord is near".

1. "Night and day we pray most earnestly that we may see you again and supply what is lacking in your faith".

1. "Since you died with Christ to the basic principles of this world, why, as though you still belonged to it, do you submit to its rules:"

1. "Finally, brothers, whatever is true, whatever is noble, whatever is right, whatever is pure, whatever is lovely, whatever is admirable – if anything is excellent or praiseworthy – think about such things".

Chapter SEVEN

AT LEAST FOUR CHARACTERISTICS EACH OF IDENTIFIED PLACES

This chapter will aid the reader improve on their ability to describe locations by particular features and distances so as to give a clear picture in the mind, leading to better understanding. Some pictures are inserted strategically to aid your understanding of information on some sites. I am however mindful of bulk thus only a few are placed. The reader can look up for more pictures in other sources.

In this chapter, names of some locations are listed. The reader is expected to supply at least four characteristics of each.

1. Bethany
2. Cana (in Galilee)
3. Macedonia (Apostle Paul in its main cities)
4. Capernaum
5. Bethsaida
6. Achaia (All of Greece)
7. Damascus
8. Galilee
9. Galatia
10. Mount Olives
11. Samaria
12. Caesarea
13. Antioch (Capital city of Syria)
14. Joppa
15. Judea (A district governed by the Romans)
16. Laodicea

17. Lydda
18. Bethlehem
19. Cilicia
20. Tarsus
21. Lystra
22. Dalmatia
23. Corinth
24. Colosse
25. Perga
26. Derbe
27. Salamis
28. Paphos (New, of the Bible)
29. Crete
30. Berea (A city in Macedonia)
31. Malta (Melita)
32. Ephesus
33. Thessalonica
34. Pamphylia
35. Pontus
36. Troas
37. Cyprus
38. Iconium
39. Antioch (A town in Pisidia)
40. Cyrene
41. Patara
42. Sidon

Chapter EIGHT

LOCATION OF MESSIANIC PROPHECIES

This chapter contains Messianic Prophecies and is aimed at making the reader know that God gave prophesies which are recorded in the Holy Bible by particular prophets in specific Bible Books. The reader is expected to **state the location of each.**

1. Would be the "seed of a woman"
2. Promised seed of Abraham
3. Promised seed of Isaac
4. Promised seed of Jacob
5. Will descend from the Tribe of Judah
6. The Heir of the Throne of David
7. Place of Birth
8. Time of Birth
9. Born of a Virgin
10. Massacre of Infants
11. Flight into Egypt
12. Ministry in Galilee
13. As a Prophet
14. As a Priest, like Melchizedek
15. His Rejection by Jews
16. Some of His characteristics
17. His Triumphant Entry
18. Betrayed by a Friend
19. Sold for Thirty Pieces of Silver
20. Money to be returned for a Potter's field
21. Judas' office to be taken by Another
22. False Witnesses Accuse Him

23. Silent When Accused
24. Smitten and Spat upon
25. Was Hated Without a cause
26. Suffered vicariously
27. Crucified with Sinners
28. Hands and feet Pierced
29. Mocked and Insulted
30. Given Gall and Vinegar
31. Hears Prophetic Words Repeated in Mockery
32. Prays for His Enemies
33. His Side to be Pierced
34. Soldiers cast lots for His coat.
35. Not a Bone to be Broken
36. To be Buried with the Rich
37. His Resurrection
38. His Ascension.

8. FULFILLMENT OF MESSIANIC PROPHECIES

The answers point the reader to fulfillment of Messianic Prophesies in the Holy Bible. Knowing them enables one to put on with the truth as seen in the time between giving of prophecy and its fulfillment.

1. But when the time has fully come God sent his

Son, born of a woman, born under the law Galatians 4:4;
Luke 2:7
Revelation 12:5

1. And you are heirs of the prophets and of the

covenant God made with your fathers. He said
to Abraham, "Through your offspring all
peoples on earth will be blessed." Acts 3:25; Matthew 1:1;
Luke 3:34

1. Abraham was the father of Isaac, Isaac

the father of Jacob, Jacob the father of
Juda hand his brothers. Matthew 1:2; Luke 3:34

1. The son of Jacob, the son of Isaac, the son

of Abraham Luke 3:34; Matthew 1:2

1. The son of Amminadab, the son of Ram, the

Son of Hezron, the son of Perez, the son of Judah Luke 3:33; Matthew 1:2-3

1. A record of the genealogy of Jesus Christ

the son of David the son of Abraham Matthew 1:1, 6

1. After Jesus was born in Bethlehem in Judea,

during the time of King Herod, Magi from the east come to Jerusalem Matthew 2:1; Luke 2:4-7

1. In those days Caesar Augustus issued a

decree that census should be taken of the entire Roman world [2](this was the first census that took place while Quinines was governor of Syria.) Luke 2:1-2,3-7

9. This is how the birth of Jesus Christ came about: his mother Mary was pledged to be married to Joseph, but before they come together she was found to be with child through the Holy Spirit. Matthew 1:18; Luke 1:26-35

10. When Herod realized that he had been outwitted by the Magi, he was furious, and he gave orders to kill all the boys in Bethlehem and its vicinity who were two years old and under, in accordance with the time he had learned from the magi. Matthew 2:16, 17-18

11. So he get up took the child and his mother during the night and left for Egypt. Matthew 2:14, 15

12. [12]When Jesus heard that John had been put in
prison, he returned to Galilee [13]leaving Nazareth
he went and lived in Capernaum which was by the
lake in the area of Zebulon and Naphtali - [14]to fulfill
what was said through the prophet Isaiah: [15]Land of
Zebulon and land of Naphtali, the way to the sea,
along the Jordan, Galilee of the Gentiles -[16]the people
living in darkness have seen a great light: on those
living in the Land of the shadow of death a light has
dawned Matthew 4:12-16

13. After the people saw the miraculous sign that Jesus
did they began to say "Surely this is the prophet who
is to come into the world". John 6:14, John 1:45
Acts 3:19-26

14. Where Jesus, who went before us has entered on
our behalf. He has become a high priest forever,

in the order of Melchizedek Hebrews 6:20

Hebrews 5:5-6, 7:15-17

15. He came to that which was his own, but his own
did not receive him John 1:11, 5:43
Luke 4:29, 17:25, 23:18

16. And Jesus grew in wisdom and stature and in
favor with God and men Luke 2:52

17. They took palm branches and went out to meet
him, shouting. "Hosanna" "Blessed is he who
comes in the name of the Lord". Blessed is the

king of Israel" ^{14}"Jesus found a young donkey
and sat upon it, as it is written." John12:13-14;
Matthew 21:1-11

18. Then Judas Iscariot, one of the Twelve, went to the
chief priests to betray Jesus to them. Mark 14:10;
Matthew 26:14-16
Mark 14:43-45

19. and asked, "what are you willing to
give me if I hand him over to you?" so they
count about thirty Silver coins for him Matthew 26:15
Matthew 27:3-10

20. the chief priests picked up the coins and said,
"It is against the law to put this in to the

treasury, since it is blood money". ^{7}So they
decided to use the money to buy the Potters field
as a burial place for foreigners. Matthew 27:6-7
Matthew 27:3-5,8-10

21. for, said Peter "it is written in the book of Psalms,
"May his place be deserted, let there be no one to
dwell in it', and, "may another take his place of
leadership". Acts 1:20, Acts 1:16-17

22. But they did not find any, though many false
witnesses came forward. Finally two came

forward^{61}and declared, "this fellow said, 'I am
able to destroy the temple of God and rebuild it
in three days,' " Matthew 26:60-61

23. Then the high priest stood up and said to Jesus

"Are you not going to answer? What is this
testimony that these men are bringing against

you?" [63]but Jesus remained silent. The high
priest said to him, "I charge you under oath by
the living God: Tell us if you are the Christ,
the Son of God". Matthew 26:62-63, 27:12-14

24. Then some began to spit at him: they blindfolded
him, struck him with their fists, and said,

"Prophesy". And the guards took him and beat him Mark 14:65

25. He who hates me hates my father as well, [24] if I
had not done among them what no one else did,
they would not be guilty of sin. But now they have

seen these miracles, and yet they have hated both

me and my father. [25]But this is to fulfill what is
written in their law: They hated me without reason'. John
15:23-25.

26. When evening came, many who were demon
possessed were brought to him and he drove out
the spirits with a word and healed all the sick.
[17]This was to fulfill what was spoken through the
prophet Isaiah:
"He took up our infirmities and
carried our diseases " Matthew 8:16-17;
Romans 4:25
1Corinthians 15:3

27. Two robbers were crucified with him one on his

right and one on his left. Matthew 27:38;
Mark 15:27-28 ;Luke 23:33

28. Then he said to Thomas "Put yourfinger here;
see my hands. Reach out your handand put it
into my side. Stop doubting and believe" John 20:27, 19:37,
20:25-26

29. Those who passed by hurled insults at him,
shaking their heads [40]and saying "You who are
going to destroy the temple and build it in three days
save yourself! Come down from the cross, if you are
the Son of God!" Matthew 27:39-40.
Matthew 27:41-44
Mark 15:29-32

30. A jar of wine vinegar was there, so they soaked a
sponge in it, put the sponge on a stalk of the
hyssop plant, and lifted it to Jesus' lips. John 19:29;
Matthew 27:34, 48

31. He trusts in God. Let God rescue him now if he
wants him, for he said, 'I am the Son of God'. Matthew
27:43.

32. Jesus said, "Father, forgive them, for they do not
know what they are doing". And they divided up
His clothes by casting lots Luke 23:34

33. Instead, one of the soldiers pierced Jesus' side
with a spear, bringing a sudden flow of blood
and water. John 19:34

34. And they crucified him. Dividing up his clothes,

they cast lots to see what each would get. Mark 15:24; John 19:24

35. But when they came to Jesus and found that he was already dead, they did not break his legs. John 19:33.

36. As evening approached there came a rich man fromArimathea, named Joseph, who had himself become a disciple of Jesus [58]Going to Pilate, he asked for Jesus' body, and Pilate ordered that it be given to him. [59]Joseph took the body, wrapped it in a clean linen cloth, [60]and placed it in his own new tomb that he had cut out of the rock. He rolled a big stone in front of the entrance to the tomb and went away. Matthew 27:57-60

37 The angel said to the women, "Do not be afraid, for I know that you are looking for Jesus who was crucified. [6]He is not here; he has risen. Just as he said. Come and see the place where he lay,

[9]Suddenly Jesus met them "Greetings," he said. They came to him clasped his feet and worshipped him. Matthew 28:5-6, 9

Luke 24:36-48.

38. When he had led them out to the vicinity of Bethany, he lifted up his hands and blessed them. [51]While he was blessing them, he left them and was taken up into heaven. Luke 24: 50- 51; Acts 1:9

CHAPTER NINE LOCATE PARABLES OF JESUS CHRIST

Some parables of Jesus Christ are listed in this chapter. The reader is expected to tell where each of these parables can be found from the Holy Bible.

1. Lamp under a bowl
2. Wise and foolish builders
3. New cloth on an old garment
4. New wine in old wineskins
5. Sower and the soils
6. Weeds
7. Mustard seed
8. Yeast
9. Hidden treasure
10. Valuable Pearl
11. Net
12. Owner of a house
13. Lost sheep
14. Unmerciful servant
15. Workers in the vineyard
16. Two sons
17. Tenants
18. Wedding banquet
19. Fig tree
20. Faithful and wise servant
21. Ten virgins
22. Talents (Minas)
23. Sheep and goats
24. Growing seed
25. Watchful servants

26. Money lender
27. Good Samaritan
28. Friend in need
29. Rich fool
30. Unfruitful fig tree
31. Lowest seat at the feast
32. Great banquet
33. Cost of discipleship
34. Lost coin
35. Lost (prodigal) son
36. Shrewd Manager
37. Rich man and Lazarus
38. Master and his servant
39. Persistent Widow
40. Pharisee and tax collector

SECTION TWO – ANSWERS

This section carry answers to questions in the nine chapters above. The reader is only expected to cross check and confirm an answer after attempts have been made at answering. The chapters are chronologically arranged just as the questions.

CHAPTER ONE FILL IN THE GAPS

1. Matthew, also known as Levi, one of the twelve

Apostles. Matthew 9:9; Mark 2:14-17;

Luke 5:27-28.

2. Word of God. Ephesians 6:17
3. Jacob's well in a Samaritan town called Sychar. John 4:4-26
4. Saul of Tarsus Acts 7:58
5. 1. Korazin
2. Bethsaida
3. Capernaum Matthew 11:20-24;

Luke 10:13-15

6. Matthias Acts 1:15-26
7. John the Baptist Matthew 14:4; Luke 3:19
8. 1. Way
2. Truth
3. Life John 14:6
9. A drink John 4:9
10. Zacchaeus Luke 19:1-9
11. Devout or Godly Acts 8:2

Stephen's site of Martyr

At the lower right hand corner of the picture is the traditional spot of the stoning of Stephen (the first Christian Martyr) Acts 7:58

12. Ten Luke 17:11-14

13. Aernon, near Salim John 3:23

14. Ephesus Acts 19:23-41

15. 1. Mary Magdalene

2. The other Mary Matthew 28:1; Mark 16:1-8;

   Luke 24:1-12; John 20:1-10.

16. Make his calling and election sure. II Peter 1:10

17. 1. Drink offering

2. Departure II Timothy 4:6

18. Master (Lord) I Peter 3:6

19. Undefiled (pure) Hebrews 13:4

20. Secret things (mysteries) of God I Corinthians 4:1

21. Meet all your needs. Philippians 4:19

22. 1. Hardness

2. Hearts Matthew 19:8

23. 1. The Lord God Almighty

2. The Lamb Revelation 21:22

24. 1. Their perseverance

2. Their faith

3. Their endurance II Thessalonians 1:4

25. 1. Unbelievers

2. Unrighteousness

3. Darkness II Corinthians 6:14

26. 1. Faith

2. Love

3. Holiness

4. Propriety I Timothy 2:15

27. Jesus Christ Acts 4:12

28. Believing Romans 10:9

29. Do nothing that would cause another stumble or

 fall in sin. Romans 14:13

30. Quarrels II Timothy 2:23

31. 1. Save that sinner's soul from death.

2. Bring about forgiveness of many sins. James 5:19

32. He lives. Romans 7:2;

 I Corinthians 7:10-11

33 1. The glory of God

2. The Lamb Revelation 21:22

34. 1. Grace.

2. Faith

3. Boast Ephesians 2:8-9

35. Faith. Ephesians 3:17

    36. 1. Christ lives in me.

2. Faith in the son of God Galatians 2:20

37. 1. Corrupted by deceitful desires

2. The attitude of their minds

3. The new self created to be like God in

true righteousness and holiness. Ephesians 4:22-24

38. 1. Denied the faith

2. Is worse than an infidel (unbeliever) I Timothy 5:39. 1. Good.

2. Finished II Timothy 4:7

40. 1. Philip

2. Andrew

3. Peter John 1:44

41. 1. Death.

2. Life John 5:24

42. 1. Steal.

2. Kill

3. Destroy. John 10:10

43. 1. Nicodemus

2. Jewish ruler John 3:1-3

44. 1. Hungry

2. Thirsty John 6:35

45. Remain in the vine (Jesus) John 15:1-4

46. 1. Faith

2. Peace Romans 5:1

47. 1. Evil

2. Understanding I Corinthians 14:20

48. Milk Hebrews 5:12-14; I Peter 2:2

49. The Lord's sake I Peter 2:13
50. 1. Critical
2. Unforgiving spirit. Matthew 6:15; Mark 11:25-26.
51. 1. Humble.
2. Like a child Matthew 18:1-5;

Mark 9:33-37; Luke 9:46-48.

52. Complaining Philippians 2:14
53. 1. Sober judgment
2. Faith Romans 12:3
54. Action I John 3:17
55. 1. Transformed by the renewing of their minds
2. What God's will is, his good, pleasing and

perfect will. Romans 12:2

56. 1. Eat
2. drink
3. whatever I Corinthians 10:31
57. 1. On your guard
2. Stand firm in the faith.
3. strong. I Corinthians 16:13
58. 1. Compassion
2. Kindness
3. Humility
4. gentleness
5. patience Colossians 3:12
59. 1. Our daily lives may win respect of outsiders.
2. so as not to be dependent on anybody. I Thessalonians 4:12
60. Crucifying the Son of God all over again. Hebrews 6:4-6
61. 1. Proud

2. Humble. James 4:6; I Peter 5:5

62. Spiritual growth Ephesians 4:31, 5:3, 4;
I Timothy 6:9, 10.

63. 1. Humbled

2. humbles Luke 14:11

Fishermen on the sea of Galilee

Fishermen on the sea of Galilee; Reminiscent of Andrew and his brother Simon Peter (Mark 1:16-20)

64. 1. Youngest

2. serves Luke 22:26

65. Lift them up. James 4:10

66. Self righteousness Luke 18:9-14; Romans 14:13

67. 1. Death

2. on the cross Philippians 2:8

68. Humility John 13:5; II Corinthians 8:9

69. The mother of my Lord Luke 1:43

70. Sixth John 4:17, 18.

71. Herod the Tetrarch Matthew 14:1-12;
Mark 6:14-29; Luke 9:7-9.

72. Bitter. Hebrews 12:15

73. A bride dressed to meet her husband. Revelation 21:2

74. Capernaum. Matthew 8:14, 15;
Mark 1:29-31; Luke 4:38, 39

75. Bartimaeus Matthew 20:29-34;

Mark10:46-52;Luke 18:35-43

76. Gadarenes Mark 5:1-15; Luke 8:26-37.

77. 1. Father

2. mother Matthew 19:5; Ephesians 4:31.

78. Ceasarea Philippi Matthew 16:13; Mark 8:27

79. Sabbath Luke 14:1-4

80. Ephraim John 11:54.

81. Beyond the Jordan John 11:39-42

82. Brothers, what shall we do? Acts 2:37.

83. Their own ungodly desires Jude 18.

84. 1. Thirty-eight

2. Sheep gate John 5:1-9

85. 1. Hearing

2. Word Romans 10:17

86. Tertullus Acts 24:1, 2.

87. 1. Judgment

2. Judgment I Corinthians 2:15

88. Faith Galatians 2:16

89. Lazarus. Luke 16:19, 20.

90. 1. Captives

2. Gifts Ephesians 4:8

91. 1. Discipline

2. Sons Hebrews 12:7

92. 1. Bread of life

2. Hungry John 6:35

93. 1. Rebellion

2. Lawlessness II Thessalonians 2:3

94. 1. Self controlled.

2. Pray. I Peter 4:7

95. The place of honor Luke 14:7-11

Island of Patmos

Island of Patmos: A place Apostle John was banished to (Revelation 1:9)

96. 1. Tail

2. Sky

3. Earth Revelation 12:1-4

97. Faith Matthew 9:27-30.

98. 1. Philip.

2. Andrew John 12:20 – 22

99. 1. An angel

2. Rolled back the stone and sat on it. Matthew 28:2

100. 1. Babylon

2. Prostitutes Revelation 17:5

CHAPTER TWO TRUE OR FALSE

S/No	True	False	Reference
1.	✓		Luke 13:10-13
2.	✓		Luke 3:2-6
3.	✓		Luke 3:25
4.	✓		Matthew 9:9; Mark 2:14; Luke 5:27
5.		✓	John 4:6 (Jacob's well)
6.		✓	Luke 10:31, 33-35.
7.	✓		John 3:1
8.		✓	Luke 17:15
9.		✓	John 2:1-11
10.	✓		John 20:26-31
11.		✓	Matthew 10:1, 11:1; Mark 6:6-13; Luke 9:1-6

12.	✓		Matthew 17:24-27
13.	✓		Matthew 21:18, 19; Mark 11:12-14, 20, 21
14.		✓	Matthew 21:28-23:29; Mark 12:1-44; Luke 20:9-21:4
15.	✓		Matthew 15:32-38; Mark 8:1-9
16.		✓	Acts 9:36-41
17.		✓	Luke 7:11-15
18.	✓		Matthew 21:18-22; Mark 11:12-14, 20-25
19.	✓		Matthew 13:3-6; Mark 4:3-6; Luke 8:5-8
20.	✓		Ephesians 6:17
21.	✓		Matthew 11:19; Luke 7:39, 19:7; John 8:11; I Timothy 1:15
22.	✓		Revelation 20:7
23.		✓	John 15:5 (branches)

24.	✓		Matthew 11:30
25.	✓		James 1:5
26.		✓	James 2:14
27.	✓		John 3:16
28.	✓		Galatians 3:28
29.	✓		Acts 22:25-28
30.		✓	Acts 9:3 (Damascus)
31.	✓		Galatians 1:17
32.	✓		Acts 17:16
33.	✓		Acts 16:14
34.	✓		Acts 17:5-8
35.	✓		Acts 16:1

36.   ✓   Acts 16:3

37.   ✓   Acts 23:12-22

38.   ✓   Acts 24:26,27

39.   ✓   Matthew 10:23

40.   ✓   Matthew 8:23-27; Mark 4:36-41

41.   ✓   Matthew 6:24

42.   ✓   Matthew 5:38-48; Romans 12:14-21

43.   ✓   Matthew 4:12,13

44.   ✓   Matthew 2:12

45.   ✓   Matthew 11:2-6

46.   ✓   Matthew 11:20-24

47.   ✓   Mathew 12:50

48.		✓	Matthew 14:26; Mark 6:49, 50; John 6:19
49.		✓	Matthew 15:22-28; Mark 7:25-30
50.	✓		Matthew 17:20
51.	✓		Matthew 18:20
52.	✓		Matthew 24:14
53.		✓	Matthew 26:69-75; Mark 14:66-72; Luke 22:54-62; John 18:15-27
54.	✓		Matthew 27:18-24; Luke 23:4, 20-25; John 19:4
55.		✓	Matthew 9:9-11; Mark 2:14-16; Luke 5:27-30
56.		✓	Mark 3:13
57.	✓		Matthew 14:3-12; Mark 6:21-29
58.	✓		Matthew 17:1-13; Mark 9:2-13; Luke 9:28-36
59.	✓		Matthew 21:12, 13; Mark 11:15-18; Luke 19:45,46; John 2:14-16

60.		✓	Matthew 22:29, 30; Mark 12:24, 25; Luke 20:34-36
61.		✓	Matthew 26:6-9; Mark 4:3, 4; Luke 7:37, 38; John 12:2, 3
62.	✓		Matthew 26:32; Mark 14:28
63.	✓		Matthew 27:32; Mark 15:21; Luke 23:26
64.		✓	Matthew 27:45; Mark 15:33; Luke 23:44
65.	✓		Matthew 1:1-16; Luke 1:27
66.		✓	Luke 1:59-63
67.	✓		Luke 2:36
68.	✓		Luke 3:23-28
69.	✓		Luke 3:28 (Bible Dictionary)
70.	✓		Matthew 5:46, 47; Luke 6:32
71.	✓		Matthew 9:20-22; Mark 5:25-34; Luke 8:43-48

72.		✓	Matthew 8:20; Luke 9:58
73.	✓		Luke 11:1-4
74.	✓		Matthew 7:13,14; Luke 13:24
75.		✓	Luke 15:28-32
76.	✓		Luke 16:20, 21
77.	✓		Matthew 21:1-7; Mark 11:1-7; Luke 19:29-35
78.	✓		Luke 19:39, 40
79.	✓		John 2:1-11
80.	✓		John 4:46-54
81.	✓		John 6:44, 65
82.	✓		John 11:45-48
83.	✓		Acts 1:18,19

84.	✓		Acts 16:16
85.	✓		I Corinthians 3:11
86.		✓	I Corinthians 6:1-8
87.	✓		I Corinthians 6:16-19
88.	✓		II Corinthians 5:20
89.		✓	Ephesians 6:12
90.	✓		Revelation 12:7
91.	✓		Philippians 2:8
92.	✓		Jude 18
93.	✓		Colossians 4:17
94.	✓		Revelation 2:19
95.		✓	I Thessalonians 5:17

96.   ✓   III John 7

97.   ✓   I Timothy 6:6

98.   ✓   I John 1:5

99.   ✓   I Peter 2:2
100.   ✓   I Corinthians 13:13

An Inn or Caravanseral

An inn or Caravanseral, with Stables for animals

CHAPTER THREE CONTEXT QUESTIONS

1. a. Apostle Peter recorded the statement.

   b. To the elect who were scattered throughout Asia Minor.

   c. To encouraging and strengthen the brethren.

   d. I Peter 5:5

   2. a. Apostle Peter recorded the statement.

   b. To the elect who were scattered throughout Asia Minor.

   c. II Peter 2:17

   3. a. The writer of the Epistle of James (probably the Lord's brother).

   b. To the Jewish converts who lived outside the Holy land (the twelve tribes scattered among the nations)

   c. James 1:15.

   4. a. Apostle Paul made the statement.

   b. To Philemon, concerning (a plea for) One sinus.

   c. Philemon 14.

   5. a. Apostle Paul made the statement.

   b. To Timothy.

   c. II Timothy 4:16

   6. a. The writer of the Epistle of James (probably the Lord's brother)

   b. To the Jewish converts who lived outside the Holy Land (the twelve tribes scattered among the nations).

   c. James 4:3.

   7. a. Apostle Paul spoke.

b. To Timothy

c. II Timothy 1:16

8. a. Apostle Paul recorded the statement.

b. To Titus

c. Titus 2:3

9. a. Apostle Paul wrote this letter.

   b. To Philemon

   c. From the prison in either Caesarea or Rome (Acts 24:27, 28:30).

   d. Philemon 21, 22.

   10. a. Apostle Paul.

   b. To Titus, Paul's son in the faith.

   c. The elect.

   d. Titus 3:1

   11. a. Apostle Paul.

   b. To the saints in Ephesus, the faithful in Christ Jesus.

   c. Ephesians 5:15.

   12. a. Apostle Paul.

   b. To the church at Philippi.

   c. When he wrote acknowledging and thanking them for their gifts.

   d. Philippians 4:12

   13. a. Apostle Paul.

   b. To Timothy.

   c. On the occasion of his advice to widows, elders and slaves.

   d. I Timothy 6:6

   14. a. Apostle Paul.

   b. To the Thessalonians church.

   c. On the occasion of his writing about men of lawlessness.

   d. II Thessalonians 2:11

   15. a. Apostle Paul.

   b. To the holy and faithful brothers at Colossi.

c. Colossians 4:2

16. a. Jesus Christ.

b. Matthew 25:13

17. a. Apostle Paul.

b. The church Apostle Paul started in Ephesus.

c. Ephesians 5:15.

18. a. Apostle Paul.

b. To the Thessalonians church.

c. The day of rapture.

d. I Thessalonians 5:4

19. a. Apostle Paul was inspired to speak.

b. The church in Colossi.

c. Jesus Christ.

d. Colossians 1:13

20. a. Apostle Paul.

b. To the Thessalonians church.

c. On the occasion of his warning against idleness.

d. II Thessalonians 3:10

21. a. On the occasion of Jesus' arrest and trial by Herod and Pilate.

b. Luke 23:12.

22. a. A man in the crowd whose son and only child was afflicted.

b. To Jesus Christ.

c. The disciples could not drive out the evil spirit.

d. Matthew 17:14-18; Mark 9:17-29;Luke 9:38-45

23. a. Apostle Paul.

b. To the church at Philippi

c. Philippians 3:14

24. a. Jesus Christ is referred to in this statement.

b. When he was being crucified on the cross of Calvary (Golgotha)

Mark 15:22; Luke 23:33

c. Matthew 27:33, 49.

25. a. Apostle Paul.

b. To the church at Thessalonica.

c. When he was explaining his ministry to the Thessalonian church

d. I Thessalonians 2:6^b

26. a. Apostle Paul.

b. Island of Malta

c. Apostle Paul shook the snake into the fire.

d. He was travelling to Rome.

Acts 28:4

27. a. Apostle Paul.

b. The church at Ephesus.

c. Ephesians 2:8, 9.

28. a. Jesus Christ is speaking.

b. Revelation 22:12

29. a. The disciples of Jesus Christ.

b. Neither the blind man nor his parents sinned.

c. Jesus spat on the ground, made some mud with the saliva, applied on the blind man's eyes and asked him to go wash in the Pool of Siloam. On obeying this instruction, he came back seeing.

d. John 9:1-7

30. a. Apostle Paul.

b. Ephesians 3:8, 9.

31. a. Apostle Paul.

b. The Corinthian Church.

c. When there was division in the church as some claimed to be his followers and others, followers of Apollo's.

d. I Corinthians 3:2.

32. a. Apostle Paul.
b. Galatians 6:7
33. a. Apostle Paul.
b. The Christians in Rome.
c. Romans 10:1
34. a. Apostle Paul.
b. The Galatians church which had been established recently.
c. Galatians 4:6.
35. a. The Christians in Rome.
b. Romans 10:9.
36. a. The works of flesh such as sexual immorality, impurity, debauchery,

idolatry, witchcraft, hatred, discord, jealously, fits of rage, selfish ambitions, dissensions, factions, envy, drunkenness, orgies and the like (Galatians 5:19-21[a]).

b. When some false preachers came attempting to convince the newly established church at Galatia to seek justification by the law rather than express their faith through love, i.e. live by the Spirit.

c. Galatians 5:1-23.

37. a. God has given Jews every opportunity and done everything possible

to get the gospel across to them but they have not responded with faith. Apostle Paul explains the gap between the gospel and man as being covered by a chain of four steps. These, being the apostles (preachers), the preaching, hearing and faith.

b. Apostle Paul.

c. Romans 10:15.

38. a. Towards the end of his correspondence to the Corinthian Church.

b. The Corinthian Church.

c. II Corinthians 13:5.

39. a. Apostle Paul.

b. The Christians in Rome.

c. Romans 6:23.

40. a. The statement was made when false apostles (preachers) came to

deceive and negate all that Apostle Paul through the power of the Holy Spirit had taught his converts.

b. Apostle Paul.

c. II Corinthians 11:13.

41. a. Apostle Paul.

b. When Apostle Paul wrote encouraging the Corinthian Church on orderly worship

c. I Corinthians 14:39, 40.

42. a. Apostle Paul.

b. To the Corinthian Church.

c. When he encouraged their generosity.

d. II Corinthians 8:11

43. a. The Christians in Rome.

b. Romans 3:23.

44. a. Apostle Paul.

b. To the new converts in Corinth.

c. II Corinthians 3:3

45. a. James.

b. When he advised on taming the tongue

c. James 3:11

46. a. Apostle Peter

b. This took place when Apostles Peter and John preached resurrection and about five thousand people prayed to receive Christ. This did not go down well with the priests, captain of the temple guard and the Sadducees who arrested the apostles. On demanding to know what power and name they preached in, Apostle Peter, being Spirit – filled gave the response which included the above statement.

c. Acts 4:12

47. a. Jesus Christ made this statement.

b. To Simon Peter.

c. When Jesus Christ washed his disciples' feet and the discussion that followed between him and Simon Peter who at first objected to his feet being washed by the Master.

d. John 13:10.

48. a. Jesus Christ spoke.

b. To his disciples.

c. At his first appearance to them after his resurrection.

d. Luke 24:44.

49. a. Apostle Paul.

b. I Corinthians 15:20.

Garden of Gethsemane

General view of the Garden of Gethsemane. A place of Jesus Christ's agony and arrest

(Matthew 26:36-56; Mark 14:32-52; Luke 22:39-54:John 18:1-12)

50. a. Judas Iscariot

b. To the crowd who came from the Chief priest, the teachers of the law and the elders armed with swords and clubs.

c. About Jesus Christ.

d. When Judas Iscariot betrayed Jesus Christ and at the point he was about to be arrested.

e. Mark 14:43-47; Matthew 26:47-56; Luke 22:42-50; John 18:3-11.

51. a. Apostle Paul made this statement.

b. When he wrote to the church at Philippi appreciating them for their gifts

c. Philippians 4:19.

52. a. Apostle Paul made this statement.
b. To Timothy.
c. I Timothy 1:12
53. a. Jesus Christ spoke.
b. To his disciples.
c. At Gethsemane.
d. When they went to pray just before he was crucified
e. Matthew 26:36-46; Mark 14:32-42; Luke 22:40 – 46
54. a. Apostle Paul
b. The church at Ephesus
c. Ephesians 6:12.
55. a. Jesus Christ spoke.
b. To some people.

c. When these people sort to know why his disciples are not fasting like the Pharisees and John's disciples.

d. Matthew 9:14-17; Mark 2:18-21; Luke 5:33-38.

56. a. Apostle Paul
b. To the church at Philippi.
c. Philippians 1:27, 28.
57. a. Jesus Christ spoke.
b. To Martha, Mary's sister.

c. Because Martha, complained to Jesus about doing on her own all the domestic work in order to entertain Jesus while her sister Mary sat listening to him without joining her.

d. Luke 10:38-42.

58. a. The Feast of Tabernacles
b. Jesus Christ.
c. He went to the temple courts and taught.

d. I. They were amazed at Jesus' acquisition of knowledge without having being schooled

ii. They accused him of demon-possession.
iii. They were angry with him for healing a man on Sabbath day.
e. John 7:10-24.
59. a. Apostle Paul
b. The Roman Christians
c. Romans 1:20

60. a. Jesus Christ presents the blood to God in heaven and obtains for man:

   i. Forgiveness
  ii. Release from bondage.
 iii. Atonement
 iv. Justification
  v. Cleansing
 vi. Holiness and victory

b. Hebrews 9:22.

61. a. Jesus Christ
b. Parable

c. Matthew 13:33

62. a. Jesus Christ

b. To his disciple

c. When about seven of his disciple led by Peter decided to go fishing after Jesus' death and resurrection

d. John 21:2, 6

63. a. Jesus Christ

b. To his disciples

c. When he sent them out on witnessing

d. Matthew 10:11

64. a. Apostle Paul spoke

b. On the occasion of his arrest in Jerusalem due to many false accusations. He was to be taken to the barracks when be requested to say something. What he said was the above quote and he spoke Aramaic.

c. They kept quiet vs. 2
   d. Acts 21:27-22:2
   65. a. The church in Thyatira
   b. Jesus Christ
   c. Revelations 2:20
   66. a. Apostle Paul

b. On the occasion of one of his series of trials after his arrest in Jerusalem. This time it was before Governor Felix who gave him audience and it was in his speech that he said this.

c. Governor Felix.

d. Acts 24:19

67. a. Apostle Paul

b. To the church at Philippi

c. Philippians 3:7

68. a. A man with dropsy

b. The Pharisees and experts of the law who closely watched Jesus Christ

c. In the house of a prominent Pharisee

d. On a Sabbath day

e Luke 14:1-4.

69. a. Apostle John (the Elder)

b. The church and her spiritual children

c. II John 12

70. a. The church in Ephesus

b. She (the church) had to her credit: perseverance enduring hardship, not growing weary and hatred for the practices of the Nicolaitans.

c. Revelation 2:1-6

71. a. It gives the believer assurance of eternal life

b. Apostle John

c. I John 5:13

72. a. Jesus Christ spoke

b. In the parable of the kingdom in which a man had good seed sown and went back to sleep only for his enemy to come and sow weeds. Jesus' disciples asked if they should

pull out the weeds, which brought their question about this
quote.

c. Matthew 13:24-30

73. a. The church in Laodicea

b. Jesus Christ spoke

c. Revelations 3:15

74. a. Apostle Paul

b. The church at Galatia

c. Eye ache

d. Galatians 4:14-16

75. a. Apostle Jude probably brother of the Lord Jesus Christ

b. Godless men (false teachers)

c. Jude 8.

76. a. Cornelius' prayer

b. An angel of God

c. He sent for Simon Peter who came, preached and baptized his
whole household.

d. Acts 10:1-48

77. a. Apostle James

b. When he advised his audience against boasting about tomorrow

c. James 4:15-16[a]

78. a. Jesus Christ spoke

b. Lazarus

c. Jesus Christ tarried where he was until Lazarus died, was
buried then he arrived four days after. He rose Lazarus from
the dead back to life (vs. 43, 44).

d. John 11:4-44

79. a. Jesus Christ spoke

b. To the crowd

c. Luke 12:54-56

80. a. Apostle John (the Elder)
b. To his friend Gaius (vs. 1)
c. III John 11

CHAPTER FOUR DIRECT QUESTIONS

1. On the mount of Olives Luke 24:44-51, Acts 1:3-9;

I Corinthians 15:7

1. At Golgotha, on a Friday Matthew 27:32-50,

Mark 15:21-41;
Luke23:26-49;
John 19:17-30

1. On the sea of Galilee Matthew 8:23-27;

Mark 4:35-41; Luke 8:22-25

1. In Bethany Matthew 26:6-13,

Mark 14:3-9,
Luke 7:36-50, John 12:1-6

1. In Galilee Matthew 10:2-4;

Mark 3:13-19;
Luke 6:12-16

1. John the Baptist, at River Jordan Matthew 3:13-17; Mark 1:9;

Luke 3:3,7, 16; John 1:28-31

1. On the sea of Galilee (Tiberius) John 21:1-25

1. The city of Jerusalem Matthew 21:1-11;

Mark 11:1-10;
Luke 19:29-44;
John 12:12-15

1. Near Bethsaida Matthew 14:13-21;

Mark 6:30-44;
Luke 9:10-17; John 6:1-14

1. In Jerusalem Matthew 21:18-19;

Mark 11:12-14

Sunrise on the Sea of Galilee

Sunrise on the Sea of Galilee

1. To strengthen what was left unfinished and

appoint elders in every town. Titus 1:5

1. Just as Jesus Christ loved the church and gave

himself up for her. Ephesians 5:25-33

13.Philip the Evangelist Acts 8:26-40

14. No, the believer should not love both God and

the world I John 2:15

15. Christians ought to live holy and godly lives II Peter 3:10-11

16. Salvation can only be obtained by grace

through faith. Ephesians 2:8-9

17. Honor your father and mother Ephesians 6:2-3

18. In Jerusalem John 7:11-52

19. According to the Book of First Timothy, a Deacon must be a man worthy of respect, sincere, not indulging in much wine, not pursuing dishonest gain, holding to the deep truth of the faith with a clear conscience and must first be tested and proven blameless. Their wives should be worthy of respect not malicious talkers but temperate and trustworthy in everything. A Deacon must be a husband of one wife, and should manage his children and household well. Those who have served well gain an excellent standing and great assurance in their faith in Christ Jesus.

The Book of Titus on the other hand says an Elder must be blameless, the husband of one wife, a man whose children believe and are not open to the charge of being wild and disobedient, not overbearing, not quick tempered not given to drunkenness, not violent, not pursuing dishonest gain, must be hospitable, love all that is good, self controlled, upright, holy, disciplined and must hold the message firmly, among others.

I Timothy 3:8-13, Titus 1:6-9

20. Healing of the royal official's son which took

place at Cana in Galilee. John 4:43-54

21. A widow should be above sixty years of age, should

have been faithful to her husband, well known for good deeds such as bringing up children, showing hospitality, washing the feet of the Saints, helping those in trouble and devoting herself to all kinds of good deeds. 1Timothy 5:9-10

22. No, God does not tempt his children James 1:13

23. Timothy's mother (Eunice) and grandmother (Lois) II Timothy 1:5

Golgotha

Traditional site of Golgotha (Matthew 27: 32-50; Mark 15:21-41; Luke 23:26-41; John 19;17-30)

24. Ruth later become an ancestor of Jesus Christ Matthew 1:5

25. The truth sets the believer free John 8:31-32

Sanctifies the believer John 17:17-19

Purifies the believer I Peter 1:22

26. Through Apostle Paul's witness I Corinthians 4:17; I Timothy 1:1

27. a. Gives the believer a sense of peace Philippians 4:6-9
b. Prepares the believer for important decision making . Luke 6:12-13

c. Strengthens believers for godly living II Corinthians 12:7-9

d. Gives the believer direction for life Acts 22:17-21

28. According to his riches in glory by Christ Jesus Philippians 4:19

29. A sycamore - fig tree Luke 19:3-4

30. The believer should practice (do) it. James 1:22

31. Because he was the product of a mixed marriage where his father was a Greek and his mother a Jew. Acts 16:1, 3

32. Elizabeth's baby leaped and Mary the mother of Jesus brought the greetings. Luke 1:39-45

33. Penetrating influence of the kingdom of God Matthew 13:33, Luke 13:21

34. Symbols of corruption and evil Matthew 16:6, 12;

I Corinthians 5:6-8;

Galatians 5:9

35. Yes, there will be use of trumpet I Corinthians 15:52;

I Thessalonians 4:16

36. There are four biographical books named:

Matthew, Mark, Luke and John.

37. a. To symbolize Christ's body and blood Matthew 26:26, 28;

John 6:51-56;

I Corinthians 10:16

b. To participate in Christ's body and blood I Corinthians 10:16

c. To remember Christ's death Luke 22:19;

I Corinthians 11:24-25

d. To proclaim Christ's death I Corinthians 11:26

e. To recall eating with the risen Lord Luke 24:30-35, 41-43;

John 21:13, Acts 1:4

f. To introduce the new covenant Matthew 26:28;

I Corinthians 11:25

g. To have fellowship with one another Acts 2:42, 46-47;

I Corinthians 11:26

h. To anticipate Christ's return Matthew 26:29;

I Corinthians 11:26

38. When his companions (Crescents and Titus) left

him for Galatia and Dalmatia respectively.

Being left with only Luke, he sent for John Mark

who came and met him there. II Timothy 4:11

39. a. The believer must glorify God I Corinthians 10:31

b. The believer must not hurt other believers I Corinthians 8:9-12;

Romans 14:13-21

1.   The believer must not use this freedom as

an excuse to sin Galatians 5:13, I Peter 2:16

40. They were four, named: Simon Peter, James, John and Andrew. Simon Peter and Andrew were sons of Jonas while James and John were sons of Zebedee and Salome. Matthew 10:2-4;
Mark 3:16-19;
Luke 6:13-16

41. Only one and is named Acts of the Apostles

42. Only one and is named Revelations.

43. On a Sabbath day Luke 13:11-13

Fishing on the Sea of Galilee

Fishing on the Sea of Galilee

44. a. For confirmation of all he had heard about

Jesus Christ.

b, He also hoped Jesus Christ would perform

some miracles for him to see Luke 23:8

45. Romans, I & II Corinthians, Galatians, Ephesians,

Philippians, Colossians, I & II Thessalonians,

I & II Timothy, Titus, Philemon. Thirteen in all.

46. James, I & II Peter, I, II & III John and Jude.

Seven in all.

47. When Jesus Christ was arrested and prosecuted Luke 23:1-17

48. Jesus Christ said, his food is to do the will of he who

sent him and to finish the work John 4:34

49. The languages of Aramaic and Greek respectively John 10:42

50. "Sovereign Lord, as you have promised, you now

dismiss, your servant in peace . For my eyes have

seen your salvation, which you have prepared in

the sight of all people, a light for revelation to the

Gentiles and for glory to your people Israel". Luke 2:29-32

51. How to be born again when a man is already old. John 3:1-4

52. For the feast of Passover Luke 2:41

53. When the water is stirred, the first person to go in is

healed of whatever disease.

It happened once a year John 5:1-9

54. No, they could not heal the boy. The boy's father

took him to Jesus Christ for healing. Matthew 17:14-18;

Mark 9:17-29; Luke 9:38-43.

55. On a Sabbath John 5:9-12

56. His native language Joh57. a. They first gave themselves to the lord such that

giving their substance became easy.

b. They received God's grace for giving II Corinthians 8:1-5

58. That they excel in the grace of giving II Corinthians 8:7

59. a. He did not deserve to have Jesus Christ under

his roof. He also counted himself unworthy to

approach Jesus Christ. He believed that Jesus

Christ could say a word and his servant will be healed.

b. That he deserved healing because he loves their

nation and has built their synagogue Luke 7:1-8

60. So that the sinful nature may be destroyed and his

Spirit saved on the day of the Lord. I Corinthians 5:1-5

61. They devoted themselves to:

a. The Apostle's teaching

b. The fellowship

c. The breaking of bread

d. Prayer

e. They were filled with awe

f. Many wonders and miraculous signs were

performed by the Apostles

g. There was sincerity of hearts

h. They enjoyed the favor of all the people

I. Shared everything in common

j. Increased daily in number. Acts 2:42-47

62. Eating and drinking judgment open oneself in the

form of sickness, weakness and even death. I Corinthians 11:29-30

63. To prevent any of them from escape by swimming. Acts 27:42

64. It is not possible. Romans 8:9

65. No, God forbid (by no means) Romans 6:1-2

66. Penitence of evil doers II Corinthians 7:8-11

67. On the account that even though bitten by a viper

from the wood that was burnt to give them warmth,

Paul neither suffered ill-effects nor did he swell up

and die. Acts 28:1-6

68. On Friday Matthew 27:27-56;

Mark 15:16-41;

Luke 23:26-49;

John 19:17-30

69. They ran out from the crowd, tore their clothes and stopped the people from sacrificing to them. Acts 14:14-18

70. By walking right through the midst of the crowd and going his way. Luke 4:30

71. On a Sabbath Luke 14:1-6

72. It was because Apostle Paul had already appealed to Caesar in Rome Acts 26:4-32, 25:11-12

73. They shouted that the gods have come down to them in human form. They therefore named Paul, 'Hermas' (Mercury) and Barnabas 'Zeus' (Jupiter). The priest of Jupiter even brought bulls and wreaths to offer to Paul and Barnabas. Acts 14:6-13

74. At the gate of the temple called Beautiful Acts 3:1-10

75. By the rolled stone from the tomb and the presence of two angels who confirmed it. Luke 24:1-5

76. Elymas the sorcerer not only opposed Paul but tried

to turn the proconsul from faith. So Paul through the

Spirit pronounced in stat on him. Acts 13:7-12

77. I. Darkness came over the whole land from the

sixth to the ninth hour

ii. The sun stopped shining

iii. The temple curtain tore into two

i. Jesus Christ called out with a loud voice

committing his Spirit in to the Father's hand. Luke 23:44-46

78. The church in Philadelphia Revelation 3:17-18

79. They secretly persuaded some men who claimed

they had heard Stephen blaspheme against Moses

and God. They then stirred up the people, elders

and teachers of the law and finally Stephen was

arrested. Acts 6:11-14

80. Because He is calling human beings to repentance Romans 2:4, II Peter 3:9, 15

81. In Bethlehem in the land of Judah Matthew 2:1, Luke 2:1-7

82. I. It flowed from the cross John 19:34

ii. It was presented to God in heaven Hebrew 9:12, 24-28

83. They were known for having a nobler

character than the Thessalonians. They

received the message with great eagerness

and examined the scriptures daily to confirm

if Paul's witness was true. Acts 17:10-11

84. He ordered the killing of all two year old boys in

Bethlehem and its environs in accordance with the

time he learned of it from the Magi. Matthew 2:16

85. I. Obedience Romans 2:25

ii. Circumcision of the heart is the true one Romans 2:28-29

iii. True worship in the Spirit of God, Philippians 3:3

 i.   Baptism i.e. the burial and rising with

Christ through faith in God's power Colossians 2:11-12

86. When he was baptized by John the Baptist at the River Jordan, the Holy Spirit came upon him just as he went out of the water.

Matthew 3:13-17;

Mark 1:9-12; Luke 3:21, 22;

John 1:31-34

Three views of the River Jordan

Three views of the River Jordan:

1. Looking downstream, showing abundant vegetation in the river gorge
2. Looking northward showing the great overhanging marl cliffs
3. A peaceful view showing the traditional site where John the Baptist carried on his Ministry and baptized his converts (Matthew 3; 6,13; Mark 1:5,9; John 1:28, 3:26; Luke 4:1)

87. They should not curse each other. James 3:9

88. Because she was kind to them as evidenced in the
robes and other dresses she made for them while alive. Acts
9:39

89. The Apostles Acts 14:23, Titus 1:5

90. a. To kill the boy Jesus Christ Matthew 2:13[b]
b. An angel of the Lord Matthew 2:13a
c. They left for Egypt as instructed by the angel
and remained there until Herod's death. Matthew 2:14-15

91. Barnabas Acts 9:27-29

92. Tabitha (Dorcas) Acts 9:36-42

93. They went there, agitated and stirred up the crowd
against Paul and his teachings. Acts 17:13

94. I. Only one baptism Ephesians 4:5
ii. Administered in water Acts 8:36-38, 10:47
iii. Essentially requiring faith Mark 16:16;
Acts 8:12, 16:31-34
iv. Requiring repentance Acts 2:38
v. Linked with receiving the Holy Spirit Acts 2:38, 10:44-48,
19:2-6
vi. Separated from receiving the Holy Spirit Acts 8:14-17
vii. Can be administered to a whole household Acts 16:15,
33;
I Corinthians 1:16

95. Because Peter had been eating with the Gentiles
until when certain men came from James, he
began withdrawing for fear of the circumcision group. Galatians 2:11-12

96. From the mouth of the fish after Jesus had instructed
him to go to the lake, throw his line into the water,
catch fish, open its mouth, take the four drachma
coin he finds there and use it to pay their tax
(that is Christ's and Peter's). Matthew 17:25-27

97. To be kind to them Luke 10:29-37
To speak the truth to them Ephesians 4:25

98. Because the allegations involved questions about
words, names and Jewish laws. Acts 18:12-15

99. Because God released huge hailstones of about one
hundred pounds weight each to fall on them.
The plague was terrible. Revelation 16:21

100. The Sanhedrin Acts 6:12-7:5
CHAPTER FIVE AT LEAST FOUR CHARACTERIS-
TICS EACH OF IDENTIFIED PERSONS

The answers to some questions number more than demanded in the
questions. The idea behind this is to guide the reader and allow freedom of choice in answering. It will also guide against controversies in
competitive situations as each answer has its scripture reference along-
side for verification.

1. a. A Christian, led by Apostle Paul to the Lord Titus 1:4

b. Gentile co-worker of Apostle Paul II Corinthians 8:23;
Galatians 2:1-3
c. Sent to Corinth II Corinthians 2:13, 8:6,16-18
d. Sent to Crete Titus 1:4-5
e. Sent to Dalmatia II Timothy 4:10
f. Companion of Paul and Barnabas on a

Journey to Jerusalem Galatians 2:1

2. a. Became an evangelist in Samaria Acts 8:5-13
b. Witnessed to and baptized the Ethiopian eunuch Acts 8:26-39
c. Continued preaching the gospel Acts 8:40
d. Had four daughters who prophesied Acts 21:9

3. a. A prophetess Luke 2:36
b. Daughter of Phanuel, from the tribe of Asher Luke 2:36
c. A young widow who continued in the worship
of God and remained a widow until she was
eighty four years Luke 2:36-37
d. Witnessed to others about baby Jesus Luke 2:38

4. a. A righteous man
Matthew 23:35, I John 3:12
b. His shed blood was considered righteous
Matthew 23:35
c. A hero of faith
Hebrew 11:4

a.   God accepted his sacrifice as better than that

of his brother Cain Hebrew 11:4

a.   Was murdered by his brother Cain Hebrew 11:4

5. a. A Christian in Rome
b. His household was greeted by Apostle Paul
c. One of the seventy disciples
d. Preached in Britain Romans16:10

6. a. A high priest when John the Baptist ministered Luke 3:2

b. Father in-law of Caiaphas the high priest John 18:13

c. Jesus was brought on trial before him John 18:13,19-23

d. Sent Jesus to Caiaphas John 18:24

e. Peter and John were brought on trial before him Acts 4:5-7

7. a. Wicked granddaughter of Herod the great Matthew 14:8

b. First married to her uncle –Philip and later
Herod Antipas Matthew 14:34;
Mark 6:17-18

c. John the Baptist reproved Herod Antipas
for his immoral act with her Luke 3:19-20; Matthew 14:3

d. Told daughter to ask for John's severed head,
on a platter Matthew 14:6-11;
Mark 6:21-27

8. a. Sister of Mary and Lazarus Luke 10:38-39

b. Kept busy in the kitchen and rebuked by
Jesus Christ Luke 10:40-42

c. Went to meet Jesus Christ after Lazarus died John 11:20

d. Confessed the resurrection John 11:20-27

e. Objected to opening Lazarus' tomb John 11:38-40

9. a. Tax collector Luke 19:1-2

b. Climbed a tree to see Jesus Christ Luke 19:3-4

c. Welcomed Jesus Christ into his house Luke 19:5-7

d. Saved by Jesus Christ Luke 19:8-9

10. a. Went with Apostle Paul on his second
Missionary Journey Acts 16:1-4

b. Stayed in Berea with Silas Acts 17:14

c. Sent to Thessalonica I Thessalonians 3:2

d. Came to Apostle Paul in Corinth Acts 18:5;
I Thessalonians 3:6

e. Sent to Macedonia Acts 19:22

f. Sent to settle problem at Corinth I Corinthians 4:17,
16:10

g. Accompanied Apostle Paul to Jerusalem Acts 20:1-4

h. Ministered to Apostle Paul in Philippi Philippians
2:19-24

i. Led the Church at Ephesus I Timothy 1:3

j. Co-writer with Apostle Paul II Corinthians 1:1;
Colossians 1:1;
I Thessalonians 1:1

k. A Pastor responsible for worship I Timothy 2:1-10;
II Timothy4:2-5

l. Was imprisoned for sometime Hebrews 13:23

11. a. A Christian woman

b. She lived in Rome

c. Greeted by Apostle Paul as "The beloved"

d. Was commended by Paul for laboring much

in the Lord Romans 16:12

12. a. Ancestor of Jesus Christ Matthew 1:1

b. His true seed is Christ Galatians 3:15-16,29

c. Rejoiced to see Jesus' day John 8:56

d. Showed greatness of Christ by giving a tithe

to Melchizedek Hebrews 7:4-10

e. Lived by faith and demonstrated it with works Hebrews 11:8-12, 17-19;

James 2:20-24

f. Believed in the power of resurrection Romans 4:17-21
g. Became father of believers Romans 4:11-12;

Galatians 3:7

h. His faith preceded the law Romans 4:9-11, 13-16; Galatians 3:17-19

i. Cast out the sons of the law Galatians4:21-31

13. a. A Pharisee and ruler of the Jews John 3:1
b. Visited Jesus Christ at night John 3:2
c. Argued for fair treatment of Jesus Christ John 7:50-52
d. With Joseph, prepared Jesus for burial John 19:38-42
14. a. Took his turn as priest in the temple Luke 1:5, 8-10
b. Received announcement of the birth of a son Luke 1:11-20
c. Could not speak for nine months Luke 1:20-22
d. Named his son, 'John'. Luke 1:59-63
e. Praised God with a song Luke 1:64-79
15. a. A Jewish believer
b. Apostle Paul's relation
c. Once a fellow prisoner with Paul
d. Paul sent greetings to him Romans 16:7

16. a. Lived in Jerusalem
b. Was righteous and devout Luke 2:25
c. Waited for the consolation of Israel

d. Sang a song of praise Luke 2:29-32

e. Prophesied concerning Jesus Christ Luke 2:34-35

17. a. A Christian woman

b. Lived in Rome and worked in the Lord

c. Known to Apostle Paul

d. Apostle Paul sent greetings to her and her

close relative. Romans 16:12

18. a. A man of Corinth

b. Apostle Paul baptized him I Corinthians 1:14

c. Hosted the church at Corinth

d. Hosted Paul and his companions Romans 16:23

19. a. One of the prophets in Jerusalem after

the persecution Acts 11:19-28

b. A prophet in the early church Acts 11:27-28

c. prophesied a severe famine for the world. Acts 11:28

d. Dramatically prophesied Paul's arrest in

Jerusalem Acts 21:10-11

20. a. An Angel Luke 1:19

b. Announced the birth of John the Baptist Luke 1:11-20

c. Appeared on the right side of the alter of

incense where Zacharias burnt incense Luke 1:11,19

d. Announced the birth of Jesus to Mary Luke 1:26-38

21. a. Brought Nathanael to Jesus John 1:44-46

b. Jesus tested him at the feeding of the five

thousand John 6:5-7

c. Introduced Greeks to Jesus John 12:20-22

d. Wanted to see the Father John 14:8-9

e. One of the Apostles Acts 1:13

22. a. Son of Alphaeus Mark 2:14

b. A tax collector Mark 2:14

c. Called by Jesus to become a disciple Matthew 9:9; Mark 2:14;

Luke 5:27

d. Also called Levi Mark 2:14-17; Luke 5:27-32

e. Held a dinner for Jesus Christ Matthew 9:10-13

23. a. A Christian in Rome

b. Loved by Apostle Paul and addressed as,

"my well beloved"

c.First convert to Christ in Achaia, the province of Asia

d. Greeted by Apostle Paul Romans 16:5

24. a. Brother of Simon Peter Matthew 4:18

b. A fisherman Mark 1:16

c. Disciple of John Baptist John 1:35-40

d. Became disciple of Jesus Christ Mark 4:18-20

e. Introduced the following to Jesus:

i. Peter John1:41-42

ii. Little boy John 6:8-9

iii. Greeks John 12:21-22

f. Asked Jesus about destruction of the temple Mark 13:3

25. a. Wife of Zechariah Luke 1:5-7

b. Relative of the Virgin Mary Luke 1:36

c. Mother of John the Baptist Luke 1:11-23, 57-58

d. Visited by Mary Luke 1:39-45

26. a. Persecuted the early church Acts 12:1

b. Killed James Acts 12:2

c. Arrested Peter Acts12:3-19

d. Died a miserable death from God Acts 12:19-23

27. a. A kinsman of Apostle Paul

b. Once a fellow prisoner with Paul

c. Became a Christian before Paul's conversion

d. Was greeted by Paul Romans 16:7

28. a. Offered a less acceptable sacrifice to God

than his brother Abel Hebrews 11:4

b. Belonged to the evil one, with evil actions I John 3:12

c. Murdered his brother Abel I John 3:12

d. Considered a symbol of evil Jude 11

e. Serve as a warning not to hate others I John 3:11-13

29. a. A Jewish believer

b. Resided in Rome

c. Loved in the Lord by Apostle Paul

d. Paul sent greetings to him Romans 16:8

30. a. Jesus Christ was compared to him Matthew 16:14

b. Appeared to Jesus in the Transfiguration Matthew 17:1-8; Mark 9:1-8

c. John the Baptist was likened to him Matthew 17:9-13;

Mark 9:9-13

d. Jesus compared his rejection to Elijah's Luke 4:24-26

e. Paul recalled a remnant in Elijah's day Romans 11:2-4

f. His prayers are examples to believers James 5:17-18

31. a. Originally called Saul Acts 13:9

b. From Tarsus Acts 9:11, 21:39

   i. From the Tribe of Benjamin Philippians 3:5

d. A Pharisee Philippians 3:5

e. Educated by Gamaliel Acts 22:3

f. Unmarried I Corinthians 7:8

32. a. One of the seven deacons Acts 6:5

b. Spoke eloquently Acts 6:8-10

c. Arrested by the Jews Acts 6:11-15

d. Gave powerful speech to the Sanhedrin Acts 7:1-53

33. a. A Roman believer

b. Resided in Rome during Apostle Paul's visit

c. Loved in the Lord by Apostle Paul

d. Paul sent greetings to him Romans 16:9

34. a. A prophet and leader of the early church Acts 15:22, 32

b. Delegated to report on council in Jerusalem Acts 15:22

c. Travelled with Paul on his Second Missionary Journey Acts 15:40

d. He shared with Paul, both the beating and imprisonment at Philippi Acts 16:19-36

e. With Paul in Thessalonica and Berea Acts 17:1-10

f. Stayed behind in Berea Acts 17:14

g. Came to Paul in Corinth Acts 18:5

h. Preached with Paul in Corinth II Corinthians 1:19

   i. Co-writer with Paul I Thessalonians 1:1;

II Thessalonians 1:1

j. Co-writer with Peter I Peter 5:12

35. a. A high priest at the time of John the Baptist Luke 3:2

b. Son in-law of Annas, the High Priest John 18:3

c. Spoke prophetically about Jesus John 11:49-53

d. Jesus was brought on trial before him Matthew 26:57-67;

John 18:24

e. Peter and John were brought on trial before him Acts 4:6

36. a. One chosen by lot to replace Judas Iscariot
to make up the Apostles' number of twelve
again Acts 1:15-26

b. Had been numbered among the followers
of Christ Acts 1:21-22

c. Was nominated along with Joseph (Barabbas,
Justus) for appointment into Judas' place Acts 1:23-26

a.   A Greek name meaning 'Gift of Jehovah'

37. a. Silversmith in Ephesus Acts 19:24

b. Incited a riot over evangelism there Acts 19:25-29

c. Told to work through legal channels Acts 19:38-40

d. Made shrines for Diana, raising much money Acts 19:24

Caiaphas' House

The Courtyard of Caiaphas' house where a Monk looks at a plaque representing a cock crowing in remembrance of Peter's denial of his Lord

38. a. A Christian at Rome

b. An approved Christian by Apostle Paul

c. Loved by Apostle Paul

d. Apostle Paul sent greetings to him. Romans 16:10

39. a. Disciple of Jesus Christ Mark 3:18

b. One of the Apostles Matthew 10:3, Acts 1:13

c. Wondered if any good can come out

of Nazareth John 1:46

d. Probably also known as Nathanael John 1:45-49

40. a. A disciple in Joppa Acts 9:36

b. Died of sickness and was laid in a room upstairs Acts 9:37

c. Raised to life by Peter Acts 9:38-41

d. A benevolent woman Acts 9:36[b], 39

41. a. Ancestor of Jesus Christ Matthew 1:1; II Timothy 2:8

b. David confessed Jesus as Lord. Matthew 22:42-45

c. Jesus sat on David's throne Luke 1:30-33

d. Was not a legalist Luke 6:1-5

e. Prophesied the Resurrection Acts 2:25-31

f. Believed righteousness comes through faith Romans 4:6-8

g. God spoke through him Hebrews 4:7

h. Jesus is the root and offspring of David

42. a. A Roman believer

b. Resided in Rome during Apostle Paul's visit

c. Loved by Apostle Paul

d. Paul sent greetings to him Romans 16:9

43. a. Roman Centurion who feared God Acts 10:1-2

b. Received vision from God Acts 10:3-8

c. Peter preached to him Acts 10:23-43

d. Received the Holy Spirit Acts 10:44-46

e. Became a baptized Christian Acts 10:47-48

44. a. Notorious criminal and prisoner at the

time of Jesus Matthew 27:16

b. Committed murder and insurrection Mark 15:7

c. Was preferred by the Jews for freedom Luke 23:18

d. Received freedom instead of Jesus Matthew 27:17-26; Acts 3:13-14; John 18:4

45. a. A Jewish Christian from Alexandria Acts 18:24

b. Instructed by Aquila and Priscilla Acts 18:26

c. Ministered at Corinth Acts 18:27-28, 19:1;

I Corinthians 3:4-9

d. Urged to revisit Corinth I Corinthians 16:12

e. Was sent by Apostle Paul to Titus Titus 3:13

46. a. Succeeded Felix as Governor Acts 24:27

b. Visited the authorities in Jerusalem Acts 25:1-5

c. Convened a court to deal with Paul Acts 25:6-12

d. Paul appealed to Caesar before him Acts 25:12

e. Consulted Agrippa about Paul Acts 25:13-22

f. Arranged an audience for Agrippa and Paul Acts 25:23-26; 29

47. a. A relative of Apostle Paul

b. A Christian in Rome

c. Loved by Apostle Paul

d. Recipient of Paul's greetings Romans 16:1

48. a. Governor of Judea Acts 23:24

b. A letter was addressed to him Acts 23:26-30

c. Paul was brought on trial before him Acts 24:1-21

d. Sought personal interview with Paul Acts 24:24-26

e. Kept Paul in prison to please the Jews Acts 24:27

Replaced by Festus

49. a. Husband of Priscilla, both tent makers Acts 18:1-3

b. Invited Paul to live with them Acts 18:3

c. Ministered at Corinth Acts 18:27-28, 19:1;

I Corinthians 3:4-9

d. Instructed Apollos Acts 18:26

e. Paul considered him a fellow worker Romans 16:3

f. Church met in their house Romans 16:4

50. a. Considered not to be married to Mary Matthew 1:18-19

a. Visited by an angel Matthew 1:20-24

c. Went to Bethlehem during census Luke 2:1-5

d. Named Mary's son, Jesus Matthew 1:25

e. Circumcised Jesus and presented him in

the temple Luke 2:21-24

f. Took Mary and Jesus to Egypt Matthew 2:13-15

g. Returned and settled in Nazareth Matthew 2:19-23

h. Went to Jerusalem for the Passover Luke 2:41-51

51. a. Seller of cloth from Thyatira Acts 16:14

b. Responded to Paul's preaching Acts 16:14

c. Invited Paul to stay in her house in Philippi Acts 16:15

d. Church met in her house Acts 16:40

52. a. Lived in Joppa Acts 9:43, 10:5, 6

b. Peter the apostle stayed with him many days Acts 9:43

c. Lived in a house by the seaside Acts 10:6

d. Peter received a vision concerning the

Gentiles in his house Acts 10:1-23

53. a. Together with his wife, they sold a possession Acts 5:1

b. Kept back part of the money Acts 5:2

c. Laid part of the money at the Apostles' feet Acts 5:2

d. Smitten of God for lying Acts 5:3-10

54. a. Disciple of Jesus Matthew 10:3; Mark 3:18

b. Ready to die with Christ John 11:16

c. Asked where Jesus was going John 14:5

d. Doubted Jesus' Resurrection John 20:24-25

e. Convinced of Jesus' Resurrection John 20:26-27

f. Confessed Jesus as lord and God John 20:28-29

55. a. A Roman

b. His household was greeted by Apostle Paul Romans 16:11

c. Besides his household, no record of his

Christianity
d.May have been a favorite freedman of Claudius
the Emperor

56. a. King who visited Festus Acts 25:13-22
b. Paul spoke before him Acts 25:23-26:23
c. Paul invited him to believe Acts 26:25-27
d. Rejected the gospel Acts 26:28
e. Declared Paul innocent Acts 26:31-32
57. a. Demonstrated God's purpose of election Romans 9:11-13
b. Was godless Hebrews 12:16
c. Sold his inheritance rightsas the eldest son

for a single meal Hebrews 12:16

d. Was rejected for not repenting Hebrews 12:17
58. a. A synagogue ruler Matthew 5:22, Luke 8:41

b. Fell at Jesus' feet and pleaded with him to
come and lay hands on his dying little
daughter so she can live again Matthew 9:18,
Mark 5:23; Luke 8:41

a.   His daughter was brought back to life by

Jesus Christ Matthew 9:25;
Mark 5:41-42;
Luke 8:54-55

d. Was encouraged by Jesus Christ to believe Mark 5:36; Luke 8:50
59. a. A Christian
b. Lived in Rome

c. Worked with other brothers

d. Apostle Paul sent his salutations to him Romans 16:14

60. a. Tetrarch of Galilee Matthew 14:1; Luke 3:1

b. Beheaded John the Baptist Matthew 14:3-12

c. Worried about Jesus Luke 9:7-9

d. Jesus Christ called him a 'fox' Luke 13:31-32

e. Participated in the trial of Jesus Luke 23:6-15

61. a. Wife of Aquila, both tentmakers Acts 18:1-3

b. Invited Apostle Paul to live with them Acts 18:3

c. Travelled with Paul to Ephesus Acts 18:18-19

d. Instructed Apollos Acts 18:26

e. Paul considered her a fellow worker Romans 16:3

f. Church met in their home Romans 16:4

62. a. The Lord called and gave him an assignment

in a vision concerning Saul Acts 9:10-17

b. Fearlessly approached Saul despite his former life of persecuting believers because he trusted the God that sent him Acts 9:13-17

c. Laid hands on Saul to restore his sight Acts 9:17-18

d. Baptized Saul Acts 9:18, 22:16

e. Commissioned Paul Acts 22:12-16

63. a. A Christian

b. Lived in Rome

c. Worked with others brothers

d. Apostle Paul sent salutations to him Romans 16:14

64. a. The Secretary of Apostle Paul Romans 16:22

b. Writer of the Epistle to the Romans as

dictated by Apostle Paul Romans16:22

c. Added his personal salutation Romans 16:22

d. Worked with Paul for sometime

65. a. Was originally named Joseph but the Apostles

   called him Barnabas Acts 4:36

   b. Sold his field and brought money to the church

   (Apostles' feet) Acts 4:37

   c. Considered a prophet, teacher and apostle Acts 13:1,14:14
   d. Brought Paul to the apostles Acts 9:27
   e. Together with Paul, brought gifts to Jerusalem Acts 11:28-29
   f. With Paul, went on missionary journey Acts 13-14
   g. Went to Jerusalem for conference Acts 15:1-2,12;

   Galatians 2:1-19

   h. Had conflict with Paul over John Mark Acts 15:36-40
   i. Had conflict with Paul over eating with Gentiles Galatians 2:11-13
   j. A fellow worker with Paul I Corinthians 9:6;

   Colossians 4:10

66. a. Only through him is Isaac's offspring reckoned Romans 9:7
   b. The one and same father of Rebecca's children Romans 9:10
   c. Shows God's purpose in election Romans 9:10-13
   d. Is an example of true faith Hebrews 11:20
67. a. The mother of James and John, sons of Zebedee Matthew 27:56; Mark 15: 40
   b. Wanted a high position for her sons Matthew 20:20-23
   c. Watched Jesus die on the cross Mark 15:40
   d. Went to the empty tomb Mark 16:1
68. a. Called 'Rock' by Jesus Matthew 16:18-19

b. Led the church in Jerusalem Acts 5:1-9

c. Paul specifically met with him Galatians 1:18

d. Spoke at Jerusalem council Acts 15:7-11

e. Called a 'pillar' Galatians 2:9

f. A party at Corinth was called by his name I Corinthians 1:12

g. Wrote two Epistles I Peter 1:1; II Peter 1:1

69. a. Samaritans considered Jacob their father John 4:7-12

b. Demonstrates God's purpose in election Romans 9:11-13

c. An example of faith Hebrew 11:21

d. Name become synonym for all Israelites Romans 11:26

70. a. Son of Simon

b. Brother of Alexander

c. A man of Cyrene

d. His mother was a mother to Apostle Paul Romans 16:13

71. a. A Corinthian

b. A City Director of Public Works

c. A believer and member of the Corinthian church

d. Also sent greetings to the Romans through

Paul's letter Romans 16:23

72. a. His birth was announced to his father Zachariah Luke 1:11-20

b. Ministered in the desert of Judea Matthew 3:1-12; Mark 1:2-8

c. Preached a baptism of repentance Luke 3:7-14;

Acts 13:24, 19:3-4

d. Witnessed concerning Jesus Christ Matthew 3:11-12;

Mark 1:7-8;

John 1:29-36

e. Baptized Jesus Christ Matthew 3:13-17;

Luke 3:21-22

f. Expressed doubts about Jesus Christ Matthew 11:2-6;

Luke 7:18-23

g. Arrested by Herod Matthew 4:12; Mark 1:14
h. Beheaded by Herod Matthew 14:1-12;

Mark 6:14-29

i. Fulfilled prophecy about Elijah Matthew 11:7-19;

Mark 9:11-13

73. a. A believer who lived in Thessalonica Acts 17:5
b. Sheltered Paul and Silas in Thessalonica Acts 17:5-7
c. Was arrested in place of Apostle Paul. Acts 17:6
d. Was among those who sent greetings from

Corinth to Rome Roman 16:21

74. a. Paul was tried before him in Jerusalem Acts 23:1-5
b. Gave order that Paul be struck on the mouth Acts 23:2
c. Was described by Paul as a white washed wall Acts 23:3
d. Was referred to as God's high priest by his

subjects Acts 23:4

75. a. A Christian woman
b. Lived in Rome and worked hard in the Lord
c. Was known to Apostle Paul
d. Apostle Paul sent greetings to her and her

close relatives Romans 16:12

76. a. A Christian

b. Lived in Rome

c. Worked with other brothers

d. Apostle Paul sent salutations to him Romans 16:14

77. a. A Christian

b. Lived in Rome

c. Worked with other brothers

d. Apostle Paul sent greetings to him Romans 16:14

78. a. Together with Peter, healed a lame man Acts 3:1-8

b. Arrested along with Peter Acts 4:1-3

c. Questioned before the Sanhedrin Acts 4:7-21

d. Sent to new Christians in Samaria Acts 8:14-17

e. Involved in the Council at Jerusalem Galatians 2:9

f. Wrote letters to 'the Elder' II John 1, III John 1

g. Exiled to Patmos Revelation 1:9

h. The prophet who wrote the Book of Revelation Revelation 1:1-33, 22:8

79. a. Appeared to Jesus at the Transfiguration Matthew 17:2-4

b. Respected for giving the law Matthew 19:7-8;

John 7:19, 23

c. Exemplified true faith Hebrews 11:24-28

d. Fore shadowed Jesus as the prophet Acts 3:21-23

e. His writings are prophetic of Jesus John 1:45

f. His lifting up of the snake showed Jesus' death John 3:14-15

g. Crossing the red sea implied baptism I Corinthians 10:1-2

h. His veil symbolized the old covenant II Corinthians 3:7-16

i. His faithfulness fore shadowed that of

Jesus Christ Hebrews 3:1-6

j. God, not Moses, gave manna John 6:30-33

80. a. Angel announced her pregnancy Luke 1:26-38

b. She visited her cousin Elizabeth and sang a song Luke 1:39-40, 46:55

c. Her virgin birth was announced to Joseph Matthew 1:18-25

d. Gave birth to Jesus in Bethlehem Luke 2:1-7

e. Presented Jesus in the temple Luke 2:21- 24

f. Fled with Joseph and baby to Egypt Matthew 2:13-15

g. Returned and settled in Nazareth Matthew 2:19-23

h. Together with Joseph, took Jesus when he was

twelve, to the Temple Luke 2:41-52

i. Had other children Mark 6:3

j. Attended a wedding in Cana John 2:1-5

k. Questioned Jesus' sanity Mark 3:21

l. Observed Jesus' crucifixion Matthew 27:55-56

m. Entrusted to John at the cross John 19:25-27

n. Among the disciples after ascension Acts 1:14

81. a. Governor of Judea John 18:28-29

b. Presided over Jesus' trial Matthew 27:11-26;

Mark 15:1-15;

Luke 23:1-5, 13-15;

John 18:28-19:16

c. Sent Jesus Christ to Herod Luke 23:6-12

d. Washed his hands as a sign of innocence Matthew 27:24-25

e. Consented to Jesus Christ's crucifixion Matthew 27:15-26;

Mark 15:6-15

a. Gave body of Jesus Christ to Joseph and

Nicodemus Matthew 27:57-60;

John 19:38-42

g. Authorized a guard at the tomb Matthew 27:62-66
h. His name forever will be associated with

Jesus' death

Acts 3:13, 4:27, 13:28;

I Timothy 6:13

82. a. A Christian
b. Lived in Rome
c. Worked with the brethren
d. Apostle Paul sent salutations to him Romans 16:15
83. a. Jesus Christ visited them Luke 10:38-39
b. Went to meet Jesus after Lazarus' death John 11:28-32
c. Listened to Jesus' teaching Luke 10:39
d. Washed Jesus' feet John 11:2, 12:1-8
e. Commended by Jesus Christ Matthew 26:6-13;

Luke 10:41-42

84. a. A member of the Jewish council Mark 15:43
b. Did not consent to Jesus' crucifixion Luke 23:51
c. A secret disciple of Jesus Christ John 19:38
d. Together with Nicodemus, prepared Jesus'

body for burial John 19:39-40

e. Buried Jesus Christ in Joseph's own tomb Matthew 27:58-60;
Mark 15:43-46;
John 19:41-42

Christ's Tomb

A close-up view of the Garden Tomb

Interior of the Garden Tomb; Supposedly the tomb from which Christ arose

85. a. Writer of the gospels of Luke and Acts

    b. A beloved brother and doctor Colossians 4:14

    c. Co-worker with Paul the Apostle II Timothy 4:11; Philemon 24

    d. Like a travel companion of Paul Acts 16:10-17, 20:5-21,

    27:1-28

86. a. Son of Zebedee and brother of John Matthew 4:21-22; Mark 3:17

    b. Originally a fisherman Matthew 4:21

    c. Wanted hostile Samaritans killed Luke 9:52-55

    d. Observed the Transfiguration Matthew 17:1-13;

    Mark 9:1-13

    e. Sought top place in Jesus' Kingdom Mark 10:35- 45

    f. Accompanied Jesus to Gethsemane Matthew 26:36-46

    g. One of the Apostles killed by Herod Acts 12:2

87. a. A Christian

    b. Lived in Rome

    c. Worked with other brethren

    d. Apostle Paul sent salutations to him Romans 16:15

88. a. Son of Zebedee and brother of James Matthew 4:21-23; Mark 3:17

    b. Originally a fisherman Matthew 4:21

    c. Uneducated Acts 4:13

d. Wanted hostile Samaritans killed Luke 9:52-55
e. Observed the Transfiguration Matthew 17:1-13;

Mark 9:9-13

f. Sought top place in Jesus' kingdom Matthew 17:1-13;

Mark 9:2-13

a.   Together with Peter, prepared a place for

the Passover Luke 22:8

h. Accompanied Jesus Christ to Gethsemane Matthew 26:36-45
i. Was called disciple whom Jesus loved John 13:23, 19:26,
20:2, 21:7, 20
j. Jesus Christ committed his mother to him John 19:26-27
k. Ran to the tomb on Easter Sunday John 20:2-8
l. Had breakfast with Jesus Christ after

his resurrection John 21:1-14

89. a. King of Judea at time of Jesus' birth Matthew 2:1
b. Was king when Zechariah was Priest Luke 1:5
c. The Magi contacted him Matthew 2:1-8
d. Ordered babies in Bethlehem killed,

on hearing of Jesus' birth Matthew 2:16

90. a. Criticized Mary for wastefulness John 12:4-5
b. Treasurer of Jesus' disciples, pilfered money John 12:6
c. Satan entered in to him Luke 22:3, John 13:27
d. Agreed with Jews to betray Jesus Matthew 26:14-16;
Mark 14:10-11

e. Betrayed Jesus Christ with a kiss Matthew 26:47-49;

Mark 14:43-45;

Luke 22:47-48
f. Identified as betrayer in the upper room Matthew 26:25;

John 13:21-30

g. Returned money to the Jews Matthew 27:3-5
h. Committed suicide and died horribly Matthew 27:5; Acts 1:18-19

i. Better not to have been born Mark 14:21

j. Called a devil and Jesus said he was doomed

for destruction John 6:70-71, 17:12

k. Replaced by Matthias Acts 1:15-26
91. a. Became sick and died John 11:2-15
b. Raised from the dead John 11:38-44
c. Present at the meal with Jesus John 12:2
d. His resurrection caused a stir John 12:17-19
92. a. Jewish name is John Acts 12:25
b. A cousin of Barnabas Colossians 4:10
c. A close friend of Peter 1 Peter 5:13
d. Believers gathered at his home to pray Acts 12:12
e. Went to Antioch with Barnabas and Paul Acts 12:25
f. Did mission work with Barnabas and Paul Acts 13:4-5
g. Deserted Paul in Pamphylia Acts 15:37-38
h. Returned with Barnabas to Cyprus Acts 15:39

i. Later became fellow worker with Paul again II Timothy 4:11;

Philemon 24

93. a. Deceitfully kept back part of their money Acts 5:2

b. Together with her husband, sold a possession Acts 5:2

c. Laid part of the money at the Apostles' feet Acts 5:2

d. Died for lying to God Acts 5:7-10

94. a. A Christian

b. Lived in Rome

c. Worked with the brethren

d. Apostle Paul sent salutations to him Romans 16:15

95. a. Former demoniac Luke 8:2

b. Supported Jesus' Ministry Luke 8:1-3

c. Present at the Cross Matthew 27:56, Mark 15:40

d. Present at Jesus' Burial Matthew 27:61, Mark 15:47

e. Went to the tomb early on Easter Sunday Matthew 28:1

f. Saw angel after the Resurrection Matthew 28:2-10;

Mark16:1-8

g. Saw Jesus Christ after the Resurrection Mark 16:9;

John 20:1-2, 10-18

96. a. Son of James Luke 6:16; John 14:22

b. Probably also called Thaddaeus Matthew 10:3, Mark 3:18

c. One of the Apostles Acts 1:13

d. Another disciple of Jesus Christ

97. a. Half brother of the Lord Jesus Christ Galatians 1:19

b. Brother of Jude Jude 1

c. Did not believe in Jesus John 7:3-5

d. Met the risen Lord I Corinthians 15:7

e. Stayed with believers before Pentecost Acts 1:13

f. Became leader of the Jerusalem Church Acts 12:17; Galatians 2:9, 12

g. Proposed solution at the Council in Jerusalem Acts 15:12-21

h. Visited by Paul Acts 21:18, Galatians 1:19

i. Wrote the Book of James James 1:1

98. a. A Christian from Cenchrea Romans 16:1

b. One of the first deaconesses if not the first of

the Christian church Romans 16:2

c. Highly recommended by Apostle Paul Romans 16:2

d. Has been a helper of many including Paul Romans 16:2

99. a. A Samaritan sorcerer Acts 8:9-11

b. Baptized as a Christian Acts 8:12

c. Offered Peter money for power to impart

the Holy Spirit Acts 8:18-19

d. Severely rebuked by Peter Acts 8:20-23

a. Received the attention of all the people in

both high and low positions of the society Acts 8:10

100. a. A Christians in Colosse

b. Believed to be the wife of Philemon Philemon 2

c. Mother of Archippus

d. Her son Archippus had no notable stability

of character Colossians 4:17

CHAPTER SIX RECITATION OF CONTENT

1. Romans Chapter Twelve, verse two (Romans 12:2)

    2. Second Peter Chapter Three, verse three (II Peter 3:3)

    3. Matthew Chapter Twenty five, verse seven (Matthew 25:7)

    4. Colossians Chapter Three, verse nine (Colossians 3:9)

    5. Hebrews Chapter Thirteen, verse seven (Hebrews 13:7)

    6. Revelation Chapter Twenty one, verse eight (Revelation 21:8)

    7. First Corinthians Chapter Ten verse twelve (I Corinthians 10:12)

    8. John Chapter Twenty, verse sixteen (John20:16)

    9. Jude verse eleven (Jude 11)

    10. Luke Chapter Nineteen, verse ten (Luke 19:10)

    11. Ephesians Chapter Five verse one (Ephesians 5:1)

    12. James Chapter Two verse seventeen (James 2:17)

    13. Second Corinthians Chapter Ten verse five (II Corinthians 10:5)

    14. Acts Chapter Seventeen verse eleven (Acts 17:11)

    15. Revelation Chapter Fourteen verses nine to ten (Revelation 14:9-10)

    16. Galatians Chapter Two, verse twenty (Galatians 2:20)

    17. Matthew Chapter Twenty six, verse fifty two (Matthew 26:52)

    18. Romans Chapter Six, verses one to two (Romans 6:1-2)

    19. Revelation Chapter Four verse eight (Revelation 4:8)

    20. Hebrews Chapter Six, verse six (Hebrews 6:6)

    21. Philippians Chapter Two, verse six (Philippians 2:6)

    22. Ephesians Chapter Five, verse fifteen (Ephesians 5:15)

    23. Acts Chapter Nine, verse six (Acts 9:6)

    24. Second Timothy Chapter Three, verse one (II Timothy 3:1)

    25. First John Chapter One verse nine (1 John 1:9)

26. Jude verse twenty (Jude 20)

27. Galatians Chapter Six, verse seven (Galatians 6:7)

28. Third John verse two (III John 2)

29. First Thessalonians Chapter Five, verses sixteen to seventeen (I Thessalonians 5:16-17)

30. Second Corinthians Chapter Five, verse seventeen (II Corinthians 5:17)

31. Second Peter Chapter Two, verse nine (II Peter 2:9)

32. Matthew Chapter One verse seventeen (Matthew 1:17)

33. Revelation Chapter Eighteen, verse four (Revelation 18:4)

34. James Chapter Four, verse seventeen (James 4:17)

35. John Chapter Eight, verse thirty two (John 8:32)

36. Mark Chapter Sixteen, verse seventeen (Mark 16:17)

37. Revelation Chapter Six, verse sixteen (Revelation 6:16)

38. Philippians Chapter One, verse twenty (Philippians 1:20)

39. Romans Chapter Eight, verse twenty eight (Romans 8:28)

40. Colossians Chapter One verse nine (Colossians 1:9)

41. Second Thessalonians Chapter Three, verse two (II Thessalonians 3:2)

42. Hebrews Chapter One, verse one (Hebrews 1:1)

43. Revelation Chapter Three, verse eleven (Revelation 3:11)

44. Acts Chapter One, verse eight (Acts 1:8)

45. Luke Chapter Twenty four, verses fifty to fifty one (Luke 24:50-51)

46. John Chapter Eight, verse forty four (John 8:44)

47. Ephesians Chapter Two, verse eight to nine (Ephesians 2:8-9)

48. Third John verse ten (III John 10)

49. Titus Chapter One verses ten to eleven (Titus 1:10-11)

50. First Corinthians Chapter Twelve, verse four (I Corinthians 12:4)

51. Acts Chapter Ten, verse thirty (Acts 10:30)

52. Revelation Chapter Seventeen, verse five (Revelation: 17:5)

53. Luke Chapter Seventeen, verse one (Luke 17:1)

54. Luke Chapter Seventeen, verse one (Luke 17:2)

55. Philemon, verse six (Philemon 6)

56. Third John verse eight (III John8)

57. First Corinthians Chapter Fourteen, verse twenty two (1 Corinthians 14:22)

58. Matthew Chapter Two, verse nineteen (Matthew 2:19)

59. Acts Chapter Two, verse forty two (Acts 2:42)

60. Titus chapter two, verse one (Titus 2:1)

61. First John Chapter Three, verse seventeen (I John 3:17)

62. Philippians Chapter Three, verse ten (Philippians 3:10)

63. John Chapter Ten, verse ten (John 10:10)

64. First Peter Chapter Five, verse seven (I Peter 5:7)

65. Romans Chapter Three, verse twenty three (Romans 3:23)

66. First Corinthians Chapter Nine, verse twenty seven (1 Corinthians 9:27)

67. Revelation Chapter Six, verse two (Revelation 6:2)

68. Galatians Chapter Two, verse twelve (Galatians 2:12)

69. Acts Chapter Eight, verse thirty (Acts 8:30)

70. John Chapter Seven, verse twenty six (John 7:26)

71. Galatians Chapter Four, verse seventeen (Galatians 4:17)

72. Second Thessalonians Chapter Three, verse sixteen (II Thessalonians 3:16)

73. Philemon verse twenty one (Philemon 21)

74. Second John verse six (II John 6)

75. Hebrews Chapter Eleven, verse one (Hebrews 11:1)

76. Philippians Chapter Four, verse seven (Philippians 4:7)

77. Titus Chapter Two, verse six (Titus 2:6)

78. Second Corinthians Chapter Three, verse two (II Corinthians 3:2)

79. Colossians Chapter Four, verse one (Colossians 4:1)

80. Romans Chapter Eleven, verse twenty nine (Romans 11:29)

81. Revelation Chapter Two, verse fourteen (Revelation 2:14)

82. First Timothy Chapter Four, verse one (I Timothy 4:1)

83. Second Peter Chapter Three, verse nine (II Peter 3:9)

84. Romans Chapter Three, verse twenty three (Romans 3:23)

85. Luke Chapter Fourteen, verse twenty seven (Luke 14:27)

86. Matthew Chapter Twenty five, verse eleven (Matthew 25:11)

87. First Timothy Chapter Five, verse one (I Timothy 5:1)

88. Hebrews Chapter Four, verse nine (Hebrews 4:9)

89. Second Peter chapter three, verse seventeen (II Peter 3:17)

90. Ephesians Chapter Six, verse ten (Ephesians 6:10)

91. First Corinthians Chapter Fifteen, verse fourteen (I Corinthians 15:14)

92. Second John verse four (II John 4)

93. Luke Chapter Ten, verse forty two (Luke 10:42)

94. Matthew Chapter Eighteen, verse twenty (Matthew 18:20)

95. Jude verse twenty two (Jude 22)

96. Hebrews Chapter Twelve, verse two (Hebrews 12:2)

97. Philippians Chapter Four, verse five (Philippians 4:5)

98. First Thessalonians Chapter Three, verse ten (I Thessalonians 3:10)

99. Colossians Chapter Two, verse twenty (Colossians 2:20)

100. Philippians Chapter Four, verse eight (Philippians 4:8)

CHAPTER SEVEN AT LEAST FOUR CHARACTERISTICS EACH OF IDENTIFIED PLACES

1. i. A town on the Mount of Olives Luke 19:29

    i.   Less than two miles from Jerusalem John 11:18
    ii. The hometown of Mary, Martha and Lazarus John 11:1
    iii. Jesus Christ stayed there after the

triumphal entry Mark 11:11
v. Jesus Christ was anointed by Mary there Matthew 26:6-13;
Mark 14:3-9; John 12:1-8
vi. Jesus Christ ascended into heaven from there Luke 24:50-51

2. i. A wedding which became so popular took

place there John 2:1

    i.   Among the guests at the wedding were

Jesus' mother, Jesus himself and his disciples John2:1-2

    i.   Here Jesus Christ performed his first miracle

of turning water into wine John 2:7-11

    i.   There he also announced to the nobleman

fromCapernaum the healing of his
apparently dying son John 4:50-54

v. Nathaniel was a native of Cana John 21:2

Bethany Village

General view of the ruins of Bethany village, less than two miles from Jerusalem (John 11:18)

3. i. Paul's had a vision of a man of Macedonia Acts 16:9

    i. Paul was in the province several times Acts 19:21, 20:1-3;

I Corinthians 16:5;

II Corinthians 1:16

    i. Some Macedonians were close to the

Apostle Paul e.g. Gaius and Aristarchus,
Secundus, Sopater and Epaphroditus Acts 17:11, 20:4;
Philippians 4:10-19;
I Thessalonians 2:8,7-20,

3:10

i. Its people were dedicated believers I Thessalonians 1:7-10;

II Corinthians 8:1-5

i. Though poor,they gave generously

for the gospel II Corinthians 8:1-4;
Romans 15:25-26

i. Helped Paul financially II Corinthians 11:7-9;

Philippians 4:14-18

4. i. Headquarters of Jesus Christ's ministry in Galilee Matthew 4:13-17; John 2:12

i. Jesus Christ taught there Mark 1:21-22; Luke 4:31-32

iii. Jesus Christ performed many miracles there:

a. Cast out demon Mark 1:21-27; Luke 4:31-37

a. Healed Peter's mother in-law Mark 1:29-31; Luke 4:38-39

c. Healed the official's son John 4:46-54
d. Healed the paralytic Mark 2:1-12
e. Healed the centurion's servant Matthew 8:5-13; Luke 7:1-10
f. Healed many people Mark 1:32-34; Luke 4:40-41
g. Miraculously brought out a coin
from the Fish's mouth to pay his
and Peter's tax Matthew 17:24-27

iv. Jesus Christ denounced it for its unbelief Matthew 11:23-24;

Luke 10:15

5. i. A town in Galilee John 12:21
ii. Three of Jesus' disciples were from there John 1:44

   i.   Five thousand people were fed there Luke 9:10-17
   ii. Jesus Christ healed a blind man there Mark 8:22-26

v. Jesus Christ denounced it for its unbelief Matthew 11:20-22;

Luke 10:13-14

6. i. A place where Paul preached to both

Jews and Greeks Acts 17:16-17, 18:4, 20:21

   i.   Location of the altar to the unknown god Acts 17:22-23
   ii. Paul's sermon to the Areopagus Acts 17:22-31
  iii. Its inhabitants wanted to speak with

Jesus Christ John 12:20-21

7. i. News of Jesus Christ went to Syria Matthew 4:24

   i.   A place where Saul went to persecute Christians Acts 9:1-2
   ii. Saul got converted near it Acts 9:3-9
  iii. Paul preached there Acts 9:19-22;

Galatians 1:17-18

   i.   Paul escaped from there in a basket Acts 9:23-25;

II Corinthians 11:32-33

Damascus' wall

the old wall of Damascus, where Apostle Paul was let down in a basket (Acts 9:23-25)

8. i. A district governed by Herod Luke 3:1, 23:5-7

   i. Jesus' disciples used to fish on its sea Matthew 4:18-22;

Mark 1:16-20

   i. Jesus Christ taught from its shore in a boat John 6:1-3, Luke 5:3
   ii. Jesus Christ walked on its sea and

stilled it's storm Matthew 8:23-27, 14:25-33;
Mark 4:36-41, Luke 8:22-26
John 6:16-21
v. Jesus Christ had an extensive Ministry there Matthew
4:23-25, 11:1;
Mark 1:14, 39; Luke 4:14-15;
John 7:1
vi. The Great commission was given in Galilee Matthew
28:16-20

9. i. A place where Paul preached the gospel Acts 16:6, 18:23

ii. Paul collected money from the Corinthian
Church I Corinthians 16:1-2

iii. Paul wrote a letter to churches there Galatians 1:2
iv. Paul wrote a letter to Christians there II Peter 1:1
10. i. Jesus Christ often went there Luke 22:39, John 8:1
ii. Jesus Christ's triumphant entry into

Jerusalem began from there Matthew 21:1-9;
Mark 11:1-10;

Luke 19:29-40
iii. Jesus Christ predicted Jerusalem's

destruction from there Matthew 24:3-34;
Mark 13:3-31

iv. Location of Gethsemane Matthew 26:30, 36;

Mark 14:26, 32

i. Location of Christ's ascension into heaven Acts 1:9-12

Mount Olives;

east view

An eastern view of the Mount of Olives; Viewed from the east wall of Jerusalem, looking across the Kidron Valley

11. i. Gospel must be preached there Acts1:8

    ii. Gospel actually spread to Samaria Acts 8:1
    iii. Philip preached there Acts 8:5-7
    iv. Holy Spirit was poured out there Acts 8:14-17
    v. Simon the magician lived there Acts 8:9-13, 18-24

12. i. A seacoast city and Roman capital of Palestine Acts 9:30,12:9-20, 18: 22,

23:23-24

ii. Philip's home and headquarters for preaching Acts 8:40, 21:8

iii. Cornelius was stationed there and Peter

preached to him there also Acts 10:1, 23-48

i. Paul was tried by King Felix and imprisoned

there for two years Acts 24:1-27

v. Paul appealed to Caesar there Acts 25:6-12

i. A Place where Paul spoke to Agrippa Acts 25:13-26:32

13. Some selected Christian events:

i. First Gentile church was located there Acts 11:19-21

ii. A place Paul and Barnabas ministered and
were sent elsewhere from there Acts 11:22-26, 13:1-3

iii. Where disciples were first called Christians Acts 11:26

iv. Agabas prophesied there Acts 11:27

v. Peter and Paul had conflict there Galatians 2:11-14

vi. The Church sent delegates to Council in
Jerusalem and received report Acts 15:1-3, 22-31

i. Paul's second and third missionary journeys

began from their Acts 15:35-40, Acts
14 .i. A place where the disciple named Tabitha
stayed Acts 9:36

ii. Simon the tanner also lived in Joppa Acts 9:43

iii. Tabitha died and was raised to life by

Peter there Acts 9:37-41

i. Peter received the famous vision which

Taughthim that the gospel was intended
for both Jews and Gentiles Acts 10:1-11:18

15. Jesus Christ and his apostles in Judea
i. Jesus was born in Bethlehem of Judea Matthew 2:1-6
ii. Jesus Christ preached in Judean synagogues

and countryside Luke 4:44, John 3:22

iii. Many people from there followed Jesus Christ Matthew 4:25;
Mark 3:8;

Luke 6:17

iv. Its residents were present at Pentecost Acts 2:5-9
v. Christians scattered throughout Judea Acts 8:1

i. Christians there suffered persecution I Thessalonians 2:14

16. i. A wealthy city in Asia Minor founded

by Antiochus II (261-246 BC)

ii. Was head of the circuit of "the Seven

Churches of Asia"

iii. Was a leading banking center as it lay on

one of the great Asian trade routes.

i. Home of a medical school and manufacture

ofcollyrium, a famous eyes salve.

i. She was "rich and increased with goods" and had

"need for nothing" Revelation 3:17

Simon the tanner's house

The roof of Simon the Tanner's house in Jaffa, ancient Joppa; A place where Apostle Paul saw a vision concerning the Gentiles (Acts 10:1-23)

17. i. Peter visited the saints in Lydda Acts 9:32

    i. Aeneas - a paralytic who had been bedridden

for eight years lived there. Acts 9:33

    i. Aeneas was healed by Peter there Acts 9:34
    ii. All who lived there saw the miracle and

turned to the Lord Acts 9:35

18. i. Known as the town of David Luke 2:4, 11
ii. Joseph, husband of Mary our Lord's mother

is from there Luke 2:4

iii. Joseph and Mary registered for the census there Luke 2:5
iv. Jesus Christ was born there Luke 2:7, Matthew 2:1

i. Shepherds visited it to worship the new born

king - Jesus Christ Luke 2:15-20

i. Here, Herod ordered the killing of all boys

two years and below Matthew 2:16-17

The village of Lydda

The village of Lydda, with the Church of St. George at the left side; Many of its residentssaw Apostle Peter's miracle of healing Aaneas and turned to the Lord (Acts 9:35)

19. i. Jews from there and environs disputed with

Stephen and conspired blasphemy against him Acts 6:8-15

ii. The gospel reached it through Paul Galatians 1:21-24
iii. Paul confirmed the church he planted there

during his Second Missionary Journey Acts 15:41

i. On his way to Rome as prisoner, Paul sailed

on the sea of Cilicia Acts 27:5

20. i. Saul's birthplace and early residence Acts 9:11, 21:39
ii. Center of a lumbering and linen industry
iii. Manufactured rough goat-hair cloth known

in the same province as Cilicium

i. During the first century before Christ, the city

was the home of a Philosophical School, a
University town where intellectual atmosphere
was colored by Greek thought.

Apostle Paul's native city

Apostle Paul's native city in Asia Minor; A street scene in Tarsus

21. i. A crippled man (lame) from birth lived there Acts 14:8

ii. The lame man listened intently to Paul and

had faith in his message Acts 14:9

iii. God healed him through Paul and he began

to walk Acts 14:10

iv. Its people mistook Paul and Barnabas for their gods and called them Hermes and Zeus respectively after the gods Acts 14:11-12

i. Its people attempted offering bulls and

wreaths to Paul and Barnabas but were stopped from during so Acts 14:13-18

vi. Paul was stoned almost to death by its people Acts 14:19-20

22. i. The word of God was brought there by Titus

when he left Apostle Paul II Timothy 4:10

ii. Was ruled by Rome as early as 160AD
iii. Was known in Paul's time as Illyricum
iv. Paul proclaimed the gospel there Romans 15:19

23. i. Apostle Paul visited if for the first time on his

Second Missionary Journey, from Athens Acts 18:1
ii. Apostle Paul began his work there with a sense of weakness, fear and trembling largely owing to the fact that he was not well received in Athens from where he was to come thereleft. I Corinthians 2:2-3
iii. A special revelation from the Lord in a night vision altered his plans to return to Thessalonica Acts 18:9-10

iv. Apostle Paul at various times sent Titus

and Timothy there I Corinthians 4:17; II Corinthians 7:13

i.   The church there responded to Apostle

Paul's appeal generously and were
commended for that II Corinthians 9:2-5

24. i. The church at Colosse was established by

Epaphras on Paul's Third Missionary Journey,
during his three years at Ephesus Colossians 1:7, 2:1

ii. Archippus exercised a fruitful Ministry there Colossians 4:17
iii. Philemon and Apphia were active members of

its church Philemon 2

iv. Tychicus and Onesimus were sent by Apostle

Paul to encourage the church there Colossians 4:7-9

25. i. The chief city of old Pamphilia in Asia minor
ii. John left Paul's company to return to

Jerusalem from there Acts 13:13

iii. Apostle Paul and his company preached

the word there Acts 14:25

iv. Apostle Paul and his team left there for Attalia Acts 14:25
26. i. A city in the south east corner of Lycaonia in

the Asia Minor
ii. Apostle Paul along with Barnabas went there
theday after he was stoned in Lystra Acts 14:20
iii. One Gaius of Derbe accompanied Apostle Paul

along with others in one of his Journeys Acts 20:4

iv. Apostle Paul visited it in his First, Second and

Third Missionary Journeys Acts 14:20, 16:1

27. i. A town on the east coast of Cyprus

ii. It had a good harbor, was a flourishing and populous town in the Hellenic and Roman periods
iii. Apostle Paul, Barnabas along with John preached the Gospel there in the Jewish synagogues Acts 13:5

iv. There was high Jewish population there

i. Though Apostle Paul did not return there

due to their disagreement, Barnabas did on his Second Missionary Journey Acts 15:39-40

vi. Barnabas was martyred there in the reign of Nero
28. i. A Roman city rebuilt by Augustus

ii. Apostles Barnabas and Paul preached the Gospel to the proconsul – Sergius Paulus there Acts 13:6-7
iii. Jewish sorcerer and false prophet named Bar- Jesus met with Apostles Barnabas and Paul there where he opposed their message Acts 13:8
iv. Apostle Paul cursed him and as a result hebecome blind. The proconsul subsequently believed Paul's message Acts 13:9-12

29. i. Apostle Paul left Titus there in order to

straighten the gospel Titus 1:5

ii. Many of the circumcision group there
turnedto be mere talkers and deceivers Titus 1:10
iii. One of its prophets described its people as
liars, evil brutes and lazy gluttons and
Apostle Paul confirmed this Titus 1:12-13
iv. Apostle Paul's ship when travelling as a
prisoner to Rome, was compelled by storm
intoits port where he warned the crew of a
pending disaster but they ignored his warning Acts 27:7-12

30. i. Apostle Paul and Silas were sent there so to

escape from a riot in Thessalonica
concerning their gospel Acts 17:5-10
ii. Apostle Paul and Silas found its people to
be more open minded and of noble character
than the Thessalonians because they studied
Paul's teachings in light of the scripture Acts 17:12
iii. Its people were however instigated by the
Thessalonians against Paul and he had to
leave for Athens Acts 17:13-15

iv. Silas and Timothy remained there and

continued to instruct the believers after
Paul fled. Acts 13:15
31 i. Though Rome acquired the island in about
218BC, the Carthaginian language was still
spoken. This explains why Luke used the
phrase "the Barbarous people" used in the
Greek sense of" "foreign speaking" Acts 28:2

ii. Was the scene of Apostle Paul's Shipwreck Acts 27:27-28:2

i.   Island said to have snakes then but not today Acts 28:3

ii. Its people were kind and hospitable Acts 28:2, 7-10

iii. Apostle Paul and the crew stayed there three

days where he healed many including the
father of his host, from sickness. Acts 28:9-10
32. i. Apostle Paul left Priscilla and Aquila there Acts 18:19
ii. Apollos learned about Christ there Acts 18:24-26
iii. God used Apostle Paul to convert some
disciples of John the Baptist there Acts 19:1-7
iv. Apostle Paul spent two years there, after which
a riot ensued concerning his evangelism Acts 19:8-41

v. Apostle Paul wrote letters to the church there Ephesians 1:1

vi. Timothy and Tychicus ministered there I Timothy 1:3;
II Timothy 4:12

i.   The Church there lost its first love Revelation 2:1-7

33. i. The second city in Europe where Apostle

Paul preached
ii. Its church was planted by Apostle Paul in his
Second Missionary Journey when he won a
reasonable population of Jews and Greeks for the Lord.
iii. The first church that received an epistle written
by Apostle Paul between 49-54 A.D.
iv. Some jealous Jews planned and rioted against
Apostle Paul such that he had to leave the city Acts 17:5-10

i.   Concerned and convinced of Christ's second

Coming, some of its people stayed idle in
wait till the Apostle Paul wrote encouraging
then to work II Thessalonians 3:11-12

34. i. A small province brought into the Roman

provincial system in the first century AD

ii. Its people were present at Pentecost Acts 2:10

iii. Apostle Paul and his companions visited the
territory on their First Missionary Journey when
he preached in one of its chief cities - Perga Acts 13:13,
14:24

iv. John Mark left the group from there and

returned to Jerusalem Acts 13:13, 15:38

i. As a prisoner Apostle Paul sailed across the

sea of Cilicia and Pamphilia Acts 27:5

i. Its inhabitants were said to be illiterate and

backward. Christianity never flourished
there as it did in other parts of Asia minor.

35. i. Jews from there were at Pentecost Acts 2:9
ii. Aquila a Jewish Christian was born there Acts 18:2

iii. Together with other Northern provinces, were
not evangelized directly by Apostle Paul as the
Holy Spirit did not permit him to preach in
Bithynia Acts 16:7

iv. Apostle Peter however addressed his first
letter to the strangers (Jewish Christians)
scattered throughout Pontus suggesting
that he preached there I Peter 1:1

36. i. Apostle Paul and his companions were

directed by the Holy Spirit to go there Acts 16:8
ii. Apostle Paul had the vision of a man of
Macedonia standing and begging him to
come to their aid. Acts 16:9-10
iii. Apostle Paul's companions went ahead at
one time and waited for him there, where
he later joined them and together, they
stayed there for seven days Acts 20:4-6
iv. Apostle Paul did not do much in it because
of Titus' absence instead he proceeded to
Macedonia II Corinthians 2:12-13
v. Brother Carpus was a resident of Troas and
Apostle Paul's host in whose place the later
left and sent for his coat and books especially
the parchments. II Timothy 4:11-12

37. i. Paphos was its capital city where the

administrator was seated
ii. In the pre-Christian era, a large colony of
Jews settled there, who later formed the
nucleus of the Christian church ministered to
by Apostle Paul and his companion
iii. At one time during the Roman rule, the Jews were
expelled from it in the days of Hadrian

iv. Barnabas and John Mark were indigenes

of Cyprus Acts 4:36; Colossians 4:10
v. Barnabas and John Mark returned to evangelize
it after parting with Apostles Paul and Silas Acts 15:36-39
38. i. A city in Asia Minor visited by Apostles
Paul and Barnabas after being expelled
fromPisidian Antioch on Paul's First
Missionary Journey Acts 13:50, 14:1
ii. Some unbelieving Jews stirred up the
Gentiles thereto mistreat and stone
Apostles Paul and Barnabas Acts14:2-5
iii. On his Second Missionary Journey, Apostles
Paul and Silas stopped there as they did the
neighboring towns, to read the letter sent out
by the Jerusalem Council Acts 16:1-2
iv. Apostle Paul alludes to persecutions endured
by him there as in Antioch and Lystra II Timothy 3:10-11

39. i. Apostle Paul preached the gospel there Acts 13:14-48
ii. Word spread from there throughout the region Acts 13:49

iii. Jews from there incited others who stirred
up persecution which sent Apostles Paul and
Barnabas out Acts 13:50-51

iv. Apostle Paul made a brief return visit to it Acts 14:21-23
v. Apostle Paul recalled persecution that

occurred there II Timothy 3:11
40. i. The Romans soldiers compelled its
native - Simon to carry Christ's Cross. Luke 23:26

ii. There people of the city were present at

Pentecost Acts 2:10

iii. Its Jewish population was large enough to

warrant citing a synagogue Acts 6:9
iv. The persecution there sent men to Antioch
preaching to the Greeks about Jesus Christ Acts 11:19-21
v. Archaeology has shown that it was the Greek
plan to make it the "Athens of Africa".

41. i. An ancient seaport of Lycia near the mouth

of the Xanthus
ii. There was an old oracle of Apollo situated there,
hence the poetic title for the god "Patareus"
iii. The trade that took place in the river valley
and its position on the Asia Minor coast made
the port important. It was convenient for ships
running East to Phoenicia or Egypt before the
prevailing autumn wind.

.

iv. Apostle Paul left for Tyre at one stage

from there Acts 21:1-2
42. i. Jesus Christ said if Sidon received so much
miracle as did Korazin and Bethsaida, it
would have repented in sack cloth Acts 11:21
ii. Jesus Christ said it will be more bearable for
Sidon on the day of Judgment than Korazin
and Bethsaida

iii. Was visited by Jesus Christ and his disciples Matthew 15:21
iv. Its people along with others were attracted to

Jesus Christ Mark 3:8; Luke 6:17-18

i. Was a residence of Christian disciples and

Apostle Paul's port of call Acts 27:3

LOCATE PARABLES OF JESUS CHRIST

1. Lamp under a bowl i. Matthew 5:14-15

ii. Mark 4:21-22
    iii. Luke8:16, 11:33

1. Wise and foolish builders i. Matthew 7:24-27

ii. Luke 6:47-49

1. New cloth on an old garment i. Matthew 9:16

ii. Mark 2:21
iii. Luke 5:36

1. New wine in old wineskins i. Matthew 9:17

ii. Mark 2:22
iii. Luke 5:37-38

1. Sower and the soils i. Matthew 13:3-8, 18-23

ii. Mark 4:3-8, 14-20
iii. Luke 8:5-8, 11-15
6. Weeds i. Matthew 13:24-30.36-43

1. Mustard seed i. Matthew 13:31-32

ii. Mark 4:30-32
iii. Luke 13:18-19

1. Yeast i. Matthew 13:33

ii. Luke 13:20-21

9. Hidden treasure i. Matthew 13:44

10. Valuable pearl i. Matthew 13:45-46

11. Net i. Matthew 13:47-50

12. Owner of a house i. Matthew 13:52

13. Lost sheep i. Matthew 18:12-14

ii. Luke 15:4-7

14. Unmerciful servant i. Matthew 18:23-34

15. Workers in the vineyard i. Matthew 20:1-16

16. Two sons i. Matthew 21:28-32

17. Tenants i. Matthew21:34-44

ii. Mark 12:1-11

iii. Luke 20:9-18

18. Wedding banquet i. Matthew 22:2-14

19. Fig tree i. Matthew 24:32-35

ii. Mark 13:28-29

iii. Luke 21:29-31

20. Faithful and wise servant i. Matthew 24:45-51

ii. Luke 12:42-48

21. Ten virgins i. Matthew 25; 1-13

22. Talents (Minas) i. Matthew 25:14-30

ii. Luke 19:12-27

23. Sheep and goats i. Matthew 25:31-46

24. Growing seed i. Mark 4:26-29

25. Watchful servants i. Mark 13:35-37

ii. Luke 12:35-40

26. Money lender i. Luke 7:41-43

27. Good Samaritan i. Luke 10:30-37

28. Friend in need i. Luke 11:5-8

The Jaffa Gate in Jerusalem's wall

*The Jaffa Gate in the wall of Jerusalem showing the 'needle's eye'.
Small doors such as this*
    *Were common features of the gates of ancient cities. Human could
pass through without problems but large animals such as camels had
to be kneel after being unloaded, in order to get through and even so,
with difficulty.*

29. Rich fool i. Luke 12:16-21
30. Unfruitful fig tree i. Luke 13:6-9

31. Lowest seat at the feast i. Luke 14:7-14
32. Great banquet i. Luke 14:16-24
33. Cost of discipleship i. Luke 14:28-33
34. Lost coin i. Luke 15:8-10
35. Lost Prodigal Son i. Luke 15:11-32
36. Shrewd Messenger i. Luke 16:1-8
a
37. Rich man and Lazarus i. Luke 16:19-31
38. Master and his servant i. Luke 17:7-10
39. Persistent Widow i. Luke 18:2-8
40. Pharisee and Tax Collector i. Luke 18:10-14

BIBLIOGRAPHY

Buursma Dirk R. N.I.V. Topical Study Bible. (Zondervan Publishing House, Grand Rapids, Michigan, USA 1998).

Frank Charles Thompson: The Chain Reference Bible, (Fourth Improved Edition. B.B. Kirkbride Bible Co., In. USA 1964).

Kenneth Barker. The N.I.V. Study Bible. (Zondervan Publishing House, Grand Rapids, MT 49530, USA 1995).

Merrill C. Tenney: The Zondervan Pictorial Bible Dictionary. (General Edition Zondervan Publishing House, Michigan 1967).

Watkins Morris and Watkins Lois. All Nations English Dictionary. (Srilanka: New Life Press

About the Author

Teryila Solomon Addi was born to the family of late Mr. Simeon Elias Ortyom and Mrs. Magdalene Hadiza Addi who have all received the supreme call to be with the Lord. He is the first of eight siblings and is in his late fifties. He was born in Kaduna, started primary school in Kano, completed in Jos and attended the prestigious N.K.S.T. Secondary School Adikpo. He worked with the Benue State Ministry of Agriculture but didn't reach the government required retirement age before leaving the service due to the Divine call into Missions. Since then, he has served in both the Para Church and Church organizations in different capacities. He holds PGDs in Animal Production, Educational Technology, Theology and a Master of Arts in Theology and Development Studies besides other short term courses and certificates. His marriage to Mrs. Shipinen Beatrice of about three decades is blessed with five children. He is currently pasturing with the Church of Christ In Nations (COCIN) and resides in Jos Plateau State.

Literature (PVT) Limited, Katunayake, 1992)

Read more at https://www.shop.otakada.org.

About the Publisher

About the Publisher – Otakada.org

Otakada.org publishing brings You Over 2,000,000 Wholesome Products and Services For The Christian Community All In One Place!

Our Passion is geared towards encouraging unity in the body of Christ and reaching Seekers and Equipping Christians in the virtual world through Evangelistic, Discipleship, Prayer and other vital Christian contents in ebooks, paperbacks, Multimedia Interactive Contents, Audio Books, Video, Magazines, News, Movies, Music and other products and services All In One Place!

Otakada Values: *Integrity, Excellence, Speed and profitability.*

Otakada Vision: *We envision a discipled world.*

Otakada Mission: *All Our resources will be geared towards discovering, harnessing and liberating Christian content for worldwide distribution and application.*

Visit https://www.otakada.org and access over 2,000,000 Christian contents on discipleship, evangelism, prayer and much more! Our Goal is to effectively engage 100 million people by 2040..stay with us. Also, Shop for goods and services, gifts and much more for the Christian community all in one place at https://shop.otakada.org!

At OtakadaValueStore.org we catering to the spirit, soul and body of Christian community and seekers all in one place.

Ingram Content Group UK Ltd.
Milton Keynes UK
UKHW020733030723
424469UK00016B/717